Are You Living Without Purpose?

The Simple Secret Nobody Tells You: How to Eliminate Anxiety

by Dennis E. Bradford, Ph.D.

Publisher's Notes

(The first edition was entitled 'What Is the Purpose of Life?')

Acknowledgements

I thank all those who personally helped me indirectly (such as The Venerable Bodin Kjolhede, Roshi, and Panayot Butchvarov), those who helped me indirectly through their works (such as Philip Kapleau, Roshi, and Eckhart Tolle), and those who helped me directly, Mark Keicher and Carlo Filice, to write this book. The truth is that it took a lifetime of experience to write it.

I alone, of course, am responsible for any and all intellectual, grammatical, or typographical errors.

Related Books by the Same Author

Introduction to Living Well

Emotional Facelift

Mastery in 7 Steps

How to Survive College Emotionally

Personal Transformation

The Three Things The Rest of Us Should Know about Zen Training

The Meditative Approach to Philosophy

Love and Respect

Getting Things Done

It's Not Just About the Money!

Table of Contents

1

❖

How to Find the Purpose of Life

There's a secret to understanding the definitive answer to the question 'What is the purpose of life?'

As long as the question is considered in isolation, it lacks a definitive answer. Why?

Since there are a multiplicity of relevant, conflicting conceptual systems to which people attach, there are a multiplicity of different answers to that question that people actually accept. For example, a Christian might think that the correct answer is to serve [his or her conception of the Christian] God. A devotional Hindu might think that the correct answer is to engage in right ritual (orthopraxy, puja). A Daoist might think it's living in alignment with the values of naturalness, equanimity, spontaneity, and freedom. An artist might think it's creating beautiful works of art. A politician might think it's obtaining and holding political power. And so on and on.

The practical result is that there is serious confusion and disagreement about what we should be doing with our lives. It's understandable that many of us simply give up seeking a definitive answer, often by postponing indefinitely, trying to answer the question.

It's good to be skeptical, questioning, about any important answer. However, it's not good simply to quit trying to understand the purpose of our lives. Such negativity merely adds to the usual heavy burden of anxiety.

Because answering the question is important, it's worth trying to answer it even though its solution is not ready-to-hand.

What is it to live well? What is it to lead a meaningful life? What is it to fulfil the purpose of life? These questions are variations on a difficult theme.

It's both important to exclude related topics as well as not to overthink this topic. For example, a related topic would be the question about the purpose of the world. To answer the question about the purpose of life is not necessarily to answer all questions about purpose. An example of overthinking would be to distinguish a meaningful life from a purposeful life by thinking about the case of a death of an infant child. We might want to say that, even though that child's life had no purpose, it was nevertheless meaningful. Let's keep this discussion as simple as possible by identifying meaning and purpose. Perhaps we might agree that such a child simply never had the opportunity to live a purposeful life.

I argue that leading a meaningful or purposeful life is opening ordinary human life to the eternal. Since the reason we fail to do that is that we have become addicted to living in our thoughts, the way to lead a life of purpose is simply to drop thoughts, which automatically opens the temporal to the eternal. Like a nonhuman animal, an infant child is already open to the eternal because that child has not yet obscured the eternal by developing the capacity to live in the human world of our own making. If so, there's no difficulty about the purpose or meaning of that infant's life.

Even if the solution is that simple, it certainly doesn't *appear* to be that simple. It's not as if, for example, we could simply look somewhere to find the answer. Jesus made this point. For him, to live well was to live in "the kingdom of God" and he said, "You cannot tell by observation when the kingdom of God comes. There will be no saying, 'Look, here it is!' or 'there it is!'"[1]

From the fact that there is no apparent solution it does not follow that there is no solution. It's true, though, that, as long as the question is considered abstractly, all there will ever be is a cacophony of answers based on different belief systems.

The reason for being optimistic about discovering a definitive answer is that these belief systems are all grounded on various different conceptions of being human. Might it be possible to agree about the nature of human being? Perhaps, but even that's unlikely.

However, what is possible is to agree about some feature of human being even if disagreement about other features remains. That, I suggest, is the way to a definitive answer to the question about our purpose.

So, *if* we could agree about a certain feature of human nature, we might agree that there is a definitive answer to the question of the purpose of human life.

There is such a feature of human nature. Linking that feature to the concept of purpose yields a definitive answer to the question of the purpose of human life.

Before considering that feature, what's not at issue here is our secondary or extrinsic purposes. Our topic is our primary or intrinsic purpose, which is the one we have simply by virtue of being human beings. Secondary purposes are roles or tasks that we adopt such as being a parent, being an author, being a carpenter, being a university student, and so on. There's nothing wrong with evaluating such purposes. They are important. Selecting those that match well with our abilities and skills is important for being happy. It's just that the purpose considered here is the one that we don't select because it's inherent in our nature.

Permit me an analogy to physics. I am not a physicist. Even if I were, physics is hardly a paradigm of knowledge; instead, it's a paradigm of rational belief. It's a system of conceptual understanding. The problem with any rational belief is that, even though it is rational, it may nevertheless be false. In the strict sense of 'knowledge,' which is the inconceivability of mistake, it is not knowledge. For example, if you were to ask a group of physicists why the expansion of the universe is accelerating, they may provide a rational guess or two, but they will ultimately just shake their heads. Is the speed of light really constant? Again, nobody really knows.

Still, using an analogy to physics may be helpful even though I must introduce another caveat: phenomenological or psychological time is not spacetime. Phenomenological or psychological time is simply time as we ordinarily experience it, as incessantly passing from the future via the present to the past. Spacetime is, supposedly, physical time, which is like a 4th dimension to ordinary three-dimensional space.

Here's the analogy: Einstein was the first to understand that, if the speed of light is constant, time itself is variable (as his familiar thought experiments suggest). Whether in fact the speed of light is constant is unimportant for the analogy: what matters is that it was part of the glory of Einstein's genius to connect the two ideas in that way.

Please consider the connection between our shared experiences of the passing of time with something constant. If something were not constant, how could we ever feel that time is passing? **What is constant cannot be time itself**. It is something "outside" time, something timeless, in other words, something eternal. Therefore, there is a feature of human being that is nontemporal.

If you are skeptical, as you should be, try thinking of it this way: if nothing were constant, we could never experience anything temporal, which is not constant. What is temporal is always in flux. Similarly, if everything in our visual field were always blue, because there'd be no contrast, we'd lack the concepts of other colors.

If so, any understanding of human nature that denies that we experience temporal flux or the flow of time would be *obviously inadequate*.

Therefore, minimally, a human being is a temporal being with a sense of the nontemporal. We have the concept of time, which means that we are able to separate that which is in time from that which is not in time.

Obviously, this is not a complete account of human nature.[2] It doesn't have to be. It's merely a necessary condition of being human. There's not only something temporal about being human, but also there's something eternal about being human at least in the minimal sense that we have the concept of time. No time, no human being. No eternity, no human being.[3]

Even if this point seems obvious, it becomes very important with respect to purpose. **To live well is to live a purposeful life**. What's that?

It's a life that is balanced between the temporal and the eternal. Why? Because living a life without balance would be ignoring a significant part of our human nature, which means that a significant part of our human nature would be automatically unfulfilled.

Words and concepts are never quite right – and those in the previous paragraph are a good example. The balance in question is not necessarily fifty-fifty like the two sides of a physical balance when the weights on each side are equal. My initial hope, though, is that the basic idea is clear: *if there are two necessary aspects (parts, sides, dimensions) of our nature (namely, the temporal and the eternal) and we ignore one, it would be impossible to live a purposeful [meaningful, fulfilled] life.*

In what follows, we'll consider the concrete implications what this means. The takeaway from this introductory chapter is this: **connecting the concept of purpose with the concept of time (temporality/eternity) is the secret key that yields a definitive answer to the question, 'What is the purpose of [human] life?'**

Our purpose is to fulfill both aspects of our nature; it is to be open to the eternal as well as the temporal.

Since everyone agrees that our lives are temporal, **in practice this means opening to the eternal**. To open to the eternal is to balance our lives between the temporal and the eternal. That's sufficient; in other words, it's unnecessary to specify how much openness to the eternal there must be.

Living well is being wise. Being wise is living a life in which the temporal and the eternal are open to each other. Being foolish, by way of contrast, is living a life that is closed to the eternal.

Sages have been saying this – although using different terminology and different conceptual systems – for thousands of years. It's not a new idea and it's not an idea original with me. If it were either, it would be shocking if the purpose of life were only discovered in the 21st century. At least if you know where to look, it's an idea that goes back at least three thousand years.

Because, though, it's so easy to get so caught up in our everyday doings that it's possible to pretend that the eternal doesn't exist, it's still a critically important idea – at least for anyone interested in living well.

So let's next determine how you can tell if you are ripe for opening to that eternal aspect of your being or if you are closed to it. After all, except possibly for reinforcement, if you are already open to it, you don't need to read this book.

2

❖

Being at Ease: Testing Yourself

Are you peaceful or is your anxiety level too high?

Living well is being at ease. Being at ease is being completely peaceful. The only humans who are completely peaceful are those who are open to the eternal. So please ask yourself: "Am I completely peaceful?" If not, it's as if poison is continually seeping into your life. It's perfectly normal not to be completely peaceful, but, in this case as in so many others, being normal is far from an optimal condition, much less the optimific condition.

Blaise Pascal: "All human misfortunes derive from one single thing, which is the inability to be at ease in a room at home."[4]

Let's use this idea to test yourself. Testing yourself is easy. Simply sit for a while, alone, in a dark and silent room where you feel safe. After a while, ask yourself, "Do I feel wholly at ease?" If not, you fail the test. However, if you fail it, don't worry, because almost nobody passes it. Why?

It's impossible to be wholly at ease while thinking. It requires alert awareness without thinking, which is sometimes called "**no-thought**" (or "no-mind"). Unless you frequently practice living without thinking, unless you frequently practice no-thought, you'll fail the test. Since most people don't do that and most of those who do practice don't do it sufficiently well, most people fail the test.

Please actually take the test. Don't settle for just reading and imagining it.

As you sit there, you will almost certainly think about lots of things. "What am I doing sitting here? How long do I have to sit here? Why can't I be cooking dinner or reading a book or watching television or cleaning the house or having sex? Wouldn't I be better off exercising or shopping?" You'll think about events that happened in the recent past. You'll think about something that may be happening elsewhere. You'll think about something that might happen in the future. And so on and on and on. You'll experience *the familiar ceaseless proliferation of thoughts*.

To think is to conceptualize. A "concept" is a principle of classification, a way of separating (sorting, dividing, categorizing). For example, to have the concept of blueness is to be able to divide objects into blue and not-blue. To have the concept of rectangularity is to be able to divide objects into rectangles and non-rectangles. To have the concept of goodness is to be able to divide objects into good and bad.

So whenever we sort or compare or contrast or evaluate we are thinking. If you are thinking as you are sitting still, you will not be completely at ease. You'll be active, mentally working.

What's wrong with that?

There's nothing necessarily wrong with thinking itself. It's a great advantage in life to be able to think. If we were unable to think, how could we solve problems? There's no serious issue about the value of thinking.

The problem comes with addiction to thinking, with the compulsion to think. There's no problem about using the mind; there's an important problem, though, about misusing the mind.

If you fail Pascal's test it's because you are addicted to thinking. Philip Kapleau makes a helpful distinction between thinking and "thoughting." Although thinking is useful, thoughting is not only useless but counter-productive.

What are the percentages? In other words, how much of our waking lives do we waste thoughting? More than one contemporary sage has said that usually about 80 or 90% of our thoughts are repetitive or stale and counter-productive. 10 or 20% of the time when we are using our minds we are thinking thoughts that are helpful, fresh, and original. It's that other 80 or 90% of thoughts that are the problem.

Answer honestly: isn't your mind out of control? Aren't you addicted to thoughting?

Even if you are, where's the problem? Besides, you may wonder, "Isn't everyone else just like me?"

It's important to understand that the problem comes from separation and, no, not everyone else is like that. It may be fair to say that, without appropriate practice or training to discipline or purify the mind, everyone else *used* to be like that and most still are. Let's consider separation in the rest of this chapter and consider what some have done to cure it in the next chapter.

People who fail Pascal's test are unable to be wholly at ease. In other words, they are dissatisfied. Something in their lives is out of balance or alignment. Their discontent may not be intense; it may only be mild. Still, what's its origin? Why are we so frequently ill at ease? Why do we so frequently feel anxiety?

Being ill at ease is being dissatisfied. It's suffering, misery, discontentment, unhappiness. It doesn't matter whether it's very mild or extremely intense. It doesn't matter what it's called. What matters is that it isn't good.

Please don't jump to the conclusion that our situation is hopeless. It's not. Why? **Dissatisfaction always has a cause**. It doesn't just happen. Since it's a condition with a cause, it's rational to hope that eliminating its cause will eliminate it.

Its origin is always the same: **separation**. It's the gap between reality, what is the case, and "surreality," what is thought to be, or ought to be, the case. That separation is always caused by thoughting, by misusing the mind. *We create dissatisfaction whenever we ask of the world what it cannot give us.* If so, obviously, once we teach ourselves not to ask for what the world cannot give, then our dissatisfaction will automatically dissolve.

Let's imagine a concrete example. Suppose that you love your mother and that, unknown to you, she just has died. How do you feel about that? Are you suffering because of her death?

No. You don't even apprehend it. Without that thought, there's no dissatisfaction.

What happens when you learn of it? You may become grief-stricken. Why? You don't want her to be dead. Her being dead isn't good for you.

Notice that the grief wouldn't exist without your apprehension of the fact of her death and also without your thought that her death is bad for you.[5] Assuming that she really did die, you would feel no loss at all without the evaluation that her death creates a permanent separation that you don't want. In that sense, it's not the reality of her death that bothers you; it's your evaluation about that situation. In that sense, you are creating the suffering yourself.

The suffering comes from the gap between thinking that mother is dead and thinking that you don't want mother to be dead. The world is not the way you want it to be. That wanting the world to be some other way than it is is what is creating your dissatisfaction, your grief, your unhappiness.

As the Stoic philosopher Epictetus wrote, "Do not seek to have events happen as you want them to, but instead want them to happen as they do happen, and your life will go well."[6] There's so much suffering in the world that it's often difficult just to watch the news on television. We often don't want the world to be the way that it is.

There's another important point here: thoughts or judgments necessarily involve separation. Therefore, they are always perspectival or partial. No single thought ever captures the whole truth, which is reality or what-is. For that reason, attaching fanatically to any single thought is foolish.

Reality is real. It is what-is. It is truth. Even if our conceptualizations of reality are only ever, at most, partial, we still need to accept or believe judgments or not. We may or may not want to believe any given judgment. Suppose for the sake of the argument that we have a judgment that is as true as it can be. Should we accept it?

Whenever we resist what is real, we lose. **Living well begins with surrendering to the reality of what-is.**

It's actually foolish not to surrender to reality. Why? It already is! We may or may not be able to improve what-is and make it more to our liking, but what-is as it is in the present moment cannot be changed. Our preferences about it, whether we like or don't like it, are irrelevant.

Sometimes, we can alleviate suffering. Often, though, there is not much that we are able to do. If your mother is dead all your wishful thinking won't bring her back.

Sometimes, though, we can alleviate suffering. For example, the oceans are warming and becoming more acidic. If that continues unabated, it's possible that all life in the oceans may collapse. Can we do something about that? At least in theory, yes. Whether it will be sufficient to prevent that catastrophe is an open question.

The Buddha is right about the best procedure for eliminating suffering. He recommends, counter-intuitively, first alleviating our own suffering before trying to help others: "Before trying to guide others, be your own guide first."[7] However, let's here resist further excursion into ethics.[8]

Please test this important idea about separation. Think of those times in your own life when you have been miserable, perhaps even suicidal. Are you able to identify the separation?

Often such times are about important losses such as loss of a lover, loss of a job, loss of a home, loss of health, and so on. Were you not miserable because you were, in effect, asking of the world what it cannot give? You were attached to one way reality should be but reality simply wasn't cooperating.

Those can be terrible times, upsetting even to recall. Please, though, recall them to learn their lesson. Life is that way, isn't it? It will try to teach us a lesson and, if we fail to learn it, it will keep repeating the same lesson until we learn it. It's important to learn the lesson about separation because the only alternative is to continue to experience it when it's not necessary to do so.

There's nothing abnormal about suffering because there's nothing abnormal about separation.

Please admit, though, that, if this analysis is correct, we are living more poorly than is necessary. In theory, suffering is optional.

In practice, it's not really wholly optional. It's perfectly normal, for example, to grieve when a loved one dies. However, and this is really good news, it's possible to minimize suffering, to reduce it dramatically.

The Buddha boils down his teaching to its essence: "what I teach is suffering and the cessation of suffering."[9] He repeatedly stresses that the chief purpose of his teaching is the elimination of dissatisfaction. "I make known just suffering and the cessation of suffering."[10]

Let's think next about how this might really be possible.

3

❖

How to Minimize Discontent

Notice that the question about the purpose of life doesn't arise when we are living well. That's an important clue. Living well, being wise, requires direct apprehension of what-is. How could that result in diminishing dissatisfaction? What's the purpose of wisdom? The Buddha's answer is, "The purpose of wisdom . . . is abandoning."[11] A sage is just someone "[w]ho clings to nothing here," in other words, someone who has detached from everything temporal.[12] What sense does this make?

It's normal to suffer, to be dysfunctional, to be unhappy, to be dissatisfied. Often life seems only occasionally punctuated by episodes of joy. Even when we are joyful, however, those moments are often bittersweet because we realize in the middle of them that they cannot last. Of course, we want them to last. We want to savor their delicious intensity forever. We sometimes cling desperately to them and, when we do, we are always disappointed. The temporal flux is relentless.

Living well is unusual, but it doesn't have to be. That's an important theme worth investigating. How can we begin living better and, perhaps, even well? The argument in the previous chapter suggests that this may be better formulated as: *How can we diminish or eliminate the separation that is causing our discontent?*

Why is living poorly normal? Why is it normal to suffer, to be dysfunctional, to be unhappy, to be dissatisfied?[13]

Why is it normal to question whether our lives have purpose?

Again, there's a cause. Living poorly just doesn't happen. So there's reason to be hopeful that, by identifying and eliminating the cause of dissatisfaction, we may be able to reduce or even eliminate it.

There's even more good news: for at least the last three thousand years some humans have not only understood the cause but figured out how to combat it. There is a way away from dissatisfaction. It's sometimes called 'the spiritual path' or 'the spiritual way' or 'the spiritual way of life.' What is it?

Sages often use the analogy to sleep to explain it. Until we awaken, we live as if asleep. **Our waking lives are like our dream lives. The solution is simply to wake up.**

Whatever we do or think in a dream is pointless. It means nothing to act or be in a certain way in a dream. A dream experience is the paradigm of a pointless experience. <u>A dream life is the paradigm of a life without purpose</u>.

<u>A fully awakened life is the paradigm of a life with purpose.</u>

Sages tell us that ordinary people, whether they are actually awake or asleep, are profoundly unaware. They assume that they are fully awake when they are not actually sleeping, but they are not. That's the root cause of all our dissatisfaction. That's why their message can be boiled down to one **prescription: wake up!** If you want to live well, wake up to reality. Wake up fully in order to stop half-dreaming through life.

What they are trying to inspire us to do is to get past or beyond thinking to profound wakefulness, which is sometimes called "superconsciousness" or "<u>samadhi</u>."

We suffer because of *how* we live. We can reduce or eliminate suffering simply by changing how we live. It's not so much that we have to change whatever we are doing; it's that we have to change *how* we are doing whatever we are doing.

How do we usually live? We are addicted to incessant thoughting. Once I've explained what this means [as in the previous chapter], I've never met an adult who didn't quickly agree. There's no issue about it.

There are only three fundamental choices: stay as we are, find something to make us less conscious, or wake up. To wake up is to open to nonconceptual, alert wakefulness or awareness. It's simply to drop all thoughts, to detach from the mind; it's beyond or past thought.

As long as our lives are not going too badly, our tendency is not to do anything, simply to adapt to dissatisfaction. We may readily admit that we are addicted to thoughting, but so what? Why change what isn't very broken? Besides, it's always a bother to change; it's always somewhat uncomfortable and sometimes very stressful. The fact is that, if we are lucky, if the degree of our dissatisfaction is relatively low, this staying as we are can work for many years, even for decades. Especially if we die young, we may be able to avoid radically changing at all.

Most of us, though, don't die before at least middle age. Nevertheless, life is short. We age more quickly than we'd like. We experience loss of health as well as other kinds of losses. We realize that, soon, we'll experience loss of life itself. The spectre of death undermines our amusements and distractions.

We may endure shocking losses that make changing easier than staying as we are. When the degree of dissatisfaction increases significantly, when suffering becomes sufficiently intense, when staying the same hurts too much, life forces us to confront the fact that there are really **only two choices**: *become less aware or more aware.*

My father, who was an internist, thought that our most serious problem as a society was to addiction to psychoactive drugs. Why do people take stimulating or intoxicating substances? Why do they take numbing substances like alcohol or heroin?

Why, similarly, do they fanatically attach themselves to the conceptual systems of others? For example, instead of thinking things through for themselves as you are doing as you work through this book, they may become religious zealots attached to religious creeds thinking that those particular thoughts will somehow magically save them (and then, often, go through life bothering other people or, even, killing those who disagree).

Are they not all attempts to feel better? At least they can sometimes deaden the suffering temporarily. Besides, becoming less aware is easy. There are many forms of readily available opium. Just pick one or more of the many available painkillers that makes you less sensitive to the question about the purpose of life. However popular this alternative, anyone who thinks that having recourse to some form of painkiller is the way to living well is a fool.

The best alternative is to do what the wise recommend. The best alternative is to wake up, which is to become more conscious, more aware, more alert. It's **the only way out of dissatisfaction that works well.** Furthermore, it's simple.

On the other hand, admittedly, it's not easy. So? Who but a fool ever thought that living well was easy? It's simple, but it's not easy. If we just let go of the thought that it should be easy, we can get on doing what is required, namely, mastering some kind of meditative or spiritual practice or training.[14]

The Buddha describes the wise, sages, as follows: "Meditating earnestly and striving for nirvana, they attain the highest joy and freedom."[15] If living well, which is sometimes called 'nirvana' or 'nibbana,' were easy, it wouldn't require much or any earnest striving. Similarly, "Hard it is to train the mind." He urges is to "Wake up! Don't be lazy." Why? That's the only way to open to living well, to "nirvana, the highest goal in life." "There can be . . . no wisdom for those who do not meditate."

Similarly, "all unwholesome states are rooted in ignorance and converge upon ignorance, and all are uprooted when ignorance is uprooted. Therefore . . . train yourselves thus: 'We will dwell diligently.'"[16] Also, "Not by means of slack endeavor, / Not by means of feeble effort, / Is this Nibbana to be achieved, / Release from all suffering."[17]

Many other sages also point out that living well, though difficult, is worth it. For example, Osho writess in Awareness: "Unless you bring total effort to waking yourself up, it is not going to happen . . . It is a long, arduous journey . . . But it is not impossible." Furthermore, "Your failures will be helpful. They can show you how unconscious you are." What do we need? "You need a 180-degree turn – that's what meditation is all about." Full consciousness not only brings goodness, but "A man of awareness is not obsessed with anything . . . He is just relaxed, calm and quiet, silent and serene." In fact, he's godly, divine.

To live well is to live in nirvana. To live in nirvana is to live in awareness rather than thought. To meditate is to practice separating awareness from thought. What is divine is living in true emptiness, which is eternity. The Buddha says that "Conceiving is a disease, conceiving is a tumor, conceiving is a dart. Therefore, bhikkhus [practitioners], you should train yourselves thus: "We will dwell with a mind devoid of conceiving."[18] Thich Nhat Hanh[19:] "True emptiness is true being." **The absence of thought is the presence of being (emptiness, eternity, nirvana, living well).**

Another way to put this is in terms of desire. The Buddha claims that [egocentric] "desire is the root of all suffering."[20] Conceiving (thinking, conceptualizing) is a necessary condition of desiring. Without separation, there'd be nothing to desire. So living well is living without desire. So living well is living without conceiving, which is living in awareness. Similarly, "with the destruction of craving comes the destruction of kamma; with the destruction of kammma comes the destruction of suffering."[21] Craving dissolves when we really come to understand that any desired "[f]orm is like a lump of foam."[22] It's foolish to desire a lump of foam because it would disappear as soon as you have it.

In his famous fire sermon, the Buddha characterizes the temporal world as "Burning with the fire of lust, with the fire of hatred, with the fire of delusion; burning with birth, aging, and death; with sorrow, lamentation, pain, displeasure, and despair."[23] It's not necessary.

Life wounds us. Why it wounds us is less important than healing the wound, which is the point of his famous analogy of a man wounded by a poisoned arrow.[24]

Why adjust to dissatisfaction when it's possible to minimize or even eliminate it?

It's true that few do this. Few live well. "Few are those among humankind / Who go beyond to the far shore. / The rest of the people merely run / Up and down along the bank."[25] Do you want to spend your life running up and down a river bank or would you rather cross over to the promised land on the far shore and live well?

The wise have been teaching us how to do this for quite a long time. Sometimes they have written books. Often, though, their most powerful teachings come from their lives, from their showing us how to live. Many, such as the Buddha and Jesus, never wrote any books. At least in the Buddha's case, that may have been because he did not want his followers to get attached to his thoughts. However, even the Buddha and Jesus used words in an effort to teach others.

Sages don't even need to use words. Their lives teach. Let's turn to a powerful familiar example that can be very instructive.

4

❖

Transition to Timelessness

S ages have had wonderful things to say about the powerful symbol of Jesus dying on the cross. Especially if you are a Christian, set aside all beliefs about it and let's do a fresh examination.

Eckhart Tolle thinks that it's such a powerful symbol of suffering that even an alien would instantly understand it. Furthermore, "Christ can be seen as the archetypal human."[26]

Let's focus here on the cross itself, which, of course, is the symbol of Christianity.

Osho, like some others, thinks of the cross as symbolizing the two dimensions of human being we've been considering, namely, the temporal and the eternal. The horizontal dimension or axis is temporal; the vertical dimension or axis is eternal. Jesus's death was moving from the horizontal dimension to the eternal dimension. It was letting go of the temporal and opening to the eternal. Applied to thought, moving from one thought to the next in a thought train is remaining in the temporal, but dropping thought altogether is moving away from the mind into the eternal.[27]

In terms of living well, the key idea is **dropping thought**, which is nonresistance.

Notice Jesus's transition from living poorly to living well. He initially resists what-is. Jesus is on the cross and cries out, "My God, my God, why hast thou forsaken me?"[28] That's the paradigm of living poorly. Then he stops resisting. He relaxes.

He says, "Father, into thy hands I commit my spirit" and dies.[29] That's the paradigm of living well, of wisdom. **The transition to the eternal is the transition from living poorly to living well**, from foolishness to wisdom.

How could a death symbolize living well? Because it's only death from the temporal side; from the nontemporal side, it's resurrection, opening to eternal life.

It's important here not to fail to distinguish between immortal life and eternal life. (That's a mistake that at least most Christians make.) Immortal life is just more temporal life, in other words, life after death (or life after life). Eternal life is timeless life. People who are greedy for immortal life are just greedy for more of the same. Although Jesus himself probably wasn't confused about this, many of his followers and translators (including Paul) certainly were. Jesus uses "the kingdom of God" to refer to eternal life. He said, "the kingdom of God is among you."[30] He wasn't talking to the dead. He was talking to the living. In other words, he was saying that the kingdom of God is available right now, right here. If you think that Christian doctrine is about the incoherent notion of immortal life, you are as confused as Paul. Jesus was talking about eternal life, which is the "true life."[31] To live well, in other words, for Jesus is to open to authentic life, true life, eternal life. It's incoherent to think that you have to wait until you are dead to do something! Opening to eternal life should be done now.

It's only the egoic mind[32] that thinks that doing that, namely, opening to the eternal, is gaining something. It's not. It's apprehending what's already available. There's nothing to gain to live well because there's nothing missing.

The task is to stop trying to gain and to open to the eternal. Do that and you'll uncover for yourself the purpose of life.

Jesus said it himself before the episode on the cross: "What will a man gain by winning the whole world, at the cost of his true self?"[33] If you focus only on your false self, you'll condemn your life to being without purpose. You'll just keep trying to gain and gain and gain more and more and more and then you'll die. On the other hand, if you focus on your true self by opening to the eternal, you will win everything valuable.

Other sages agree. For example, many Buddhist sages tell us that there is nothing to gain. Sengcan, the third Zen ancestor and the author of the oldest extant Zen document from ancient China writes: "The wise do not strive after goals."[34] Why not? There's no goal worth attaining.

Sengcan recommends getting rid of gain and loss. Why? To live trying gain something (such as money or sex or power or prestige) is to live with motivation. It's extrinsic motivation, which has a purpose, a point, or a goal. To live with motivation is to attempt to gain something. Stop living like that. To live without motivation is to live without attempting to gain anything. It's intrinsic motivation, which lacks a purpose, a point, or a goal. There's no goal worth your life. There's nothing important to gain.

It *seems* paradoxical: **to give up purpose is to open to purposeful living**. The key to understanding it is to accept both the temporality and the eternality of human nature. Once that is accepted, the apparent paradox disappears.

As temporal beings we have certain needs such as food. When we lack them, gaining them is good. However, if all we do is focus on what we need or want, we miss what is most valuable, namely, opening to the eternal. Living is temporal, but living well requires opening to what is not temporal. In that sense, living well is a balance between the temporal and the eternal.

Do you live with a clinging mind that seeks to attach? Or do you live without clinging and without seeking to attach? If the former, Sengcan's advice is: "Just let go now of clinging mind." Drop mind altogether. In other words, detach from thoughts, which are a "heavy burden" that weigh us down. Until we stop living in bondage to our thoughts, we'll always be "confused, unclear." Until we stop living solely as an effort to do things, to achieve goals, we'll remain fools in bondage to our thoughts.

It's important to realize that this includes seeking awakening (spiritual enlightenment). Unlike the temporal, the eternal cannot be thought or conceptualized. Therefore, it's impossible to think our way to the eternal. Seeking it "with thinking mind is certainly a grave mistake." Seeking what we want and trying to avoid what we don't want is "the mind's disease." Genuine well-being lies in the domain beyond or past thought. There's no need to seek it. Why?

We already *are* it. The reason that we don't realize it is because our apprehension of it is obstructed by thoughts.

There's no complicated theory to understand. There's no creed to memorize and swear allegiance to. There's no thought that is required for wisdom. There's nothing to learn. There's nothing to search for. There's no task to be accomplished. There's nothing to be gained.

Awakening is simply letting go of all thoughts. That means dropping all sorting, conceptualizing, comparing, and evaluating. Living an awakened life means doing that moment by moment.

Actually, it can be very misleading to think in terms of an awakened life.[35] It's easier and less misleading to think in terms of a single episode. Let's do that because it will demonstrate how mind or thought works.

Imagine seeing a spectacular sunset. Let's say that you are camping in the western mountains and the meteorological conditions are such that you happen to look up and are confronted with a glorious view.

It just confronts you. You are facing it. It's stunningly beautiful. It's a wholly passive experience. It's simply witnessing of one of Mother Nature's glories. This is a perfectly familiar kind of example, isn't it?

Now let's change it: let's think about it. You make a judgment, a conceptualization. Thinking of it, you say or think: "That's a beautiful sunset." What have you done?

Notice, first, that you have done something. Thinking is mental doing. Again, it's sorting or classifying. You have conceptualized it.

Notice, second, that you have brought the past into the present moment. Why? When did you learn the concept of beauty? Years ago. Same with the concept of a sunset. You learned all the words and concepts you use now in the past, didn't you? So what you have done is to contaminate the direct experience of seeing that beautiful sunset in the present moment with concepts (namely, being a sunset and being beautiful) that you learned in the past. By doing that, obviously you have changed the passive experience to an active one. Mind stuff is past stuff. To bring mind into the present contaminates the present with the past. Doing that deadens the experience. It kills its vitality and freshness. There's nothing that needs to be understood in the present moment. Observing the sunset and appreciating its beauty doesn't require any thinking at all.

Notice, third, that thinking your present experience is thinking "I'm seeing a beautiful sunset." That also brings the concept of self or ego into the experience. As explained in the following chapter, that's a very bad move.

In short, **there's nothing to do**. As soon as you think about the experience, you diminish it. Make a habit of doing that, as we all do until we teach ourselves how to live better, and you'll accomplish nothing except diminishing the quality of your life by diminishing the quality of your experiences.

That's how we turn pain into dissatisfaction (suffering). Pain is natural. Since it has survival value, it's likely that all sentient beings experience pain at least occasionally. (The same goes for pleasure.) So, how should we proceed when we feel pain? Accept it. It happens. If it's worth trying to do so, minimize or eliminate it. If you break a leg, stop walking on it to allow it to heal. The main point, though, is to let it go, in other words, stop thinking about it. The more we focus on an experience, the more its importance intensifies. If you focus on pain, it only feels worse. Instead of simply admitting this and living accordingly, don't we often do exactly the opposite? Don't we take a pain and intensify it? "Oh, woe is me! Why am I always the one who gets injured? Why do these kinds of things only happen to me?" When I have a stomach ache, instead of just having a pain, if I think about it enough I can actually turn it into an illness with a prolonged temporal duration, a beginning, middle, and end. Aren't you beginning to imagine hearing the endless complaints?

Although you may just have realized this for the first time, this is not a new thought. Sages have pointed it out. In <u>Awareness</u>, for example, Osho writes: "truth is virgin." *There's no need to go through life incessantly judging and evaluating everything.* That's nothing but a terrible habit that we have that prevents us from living well. You'll enjoy the sunset more if you don't drag the past into it: just gaze in silent, thoughtless awe.

At least when you don't have to do something, just be. Sengcan: "Abide not in duality; refrain from all pursuit of it."

What happens when we stop thinking and stop clinging?

Sengcan is perfectly clear: "If all thought-objects disappear, the thinking subject drops away." Aha! Here's another topic worthy of investigation: the self. Before turning to it in the next chapter, please notice two additional points related to this quotation.

Please notice first that he is explicitly only talking about the disappearance of "thought-objects." He's not talking about the disappearance of all objects. To continue the same example, the sunset is an object; it's something we're singling out for attention, something we're paying attention to. In this case it's something that we're seeing, which is a way of perceiving. There is, in other words, an episode of consciousness about something, namely, the sunset. We turn that object, the sunset, into a thought-object when we begin thinking about it, as we would do if we thought, "I am seeing a sunset." Again, this is how the ego (self, the egoic mind) becomes part of experience: we bring it in. There's no need to do that. As soon as we do it, objects become thought-objects. That's critical because it's the transition from living in the world to living in our thoughts.

The second point concerns what he also says: "When all is seen with 'equal mind,' to our Self-nature we return."

This is the problem with thought-objects: they are not just objects. An object (form, thing) is something singled out for attention. When we switch from awareness of objects to conceptualizing or judging thought-objects, we are discriminating and creating inequality. Remember: thinking is sorting or classifying. The thoughtful or egoic mind creates separation and inequality that uncontaminated awareness of objects lacks. Where 'x' is a variable that ranges over objects and 'F' denotes some concept or other, the difference here is the simply the difference between 'x' and 'x is F' (or 'x is y' if it's an identity judgment rather than a predication). In the case of the sunset, this inequality, this difference between x and x is F may seem innocuous. After all, what we are really doing when we think about it is undermining the quality of the sunset, which is only hurting us.

That's initially true. However, that was just one experience. How many experiences do you have in the course of a single waking day? How many experiences do you have in a week or a month or a year or a decade or a lifetime? Incessant thought creates ubiquitous inequality and the effects of that sooner or later always have an impact on others. The diminished quality of our own lives inevitably eventually affects others negatively.

What Sengcan is recommending is a transition from self to Self. Our Self is natural. It's also without separation. It may be thought of as unity, but, of course, since it's beyond thought, thinking of it as anything is never correct. The point of mentioning unity is because there is no separation in unity. **Because dissatisfaction comes from separation and there is no separation without thought, dropping thought eliminates separation and, so, dissatisfaction.** This is the connection between thinking and living well.

Another way to put this is to admit that, when we think, we change objects into thought-objects. This is how we transition from living in the world to living in our thoughts. *We create separation where there isn't any.* The reason this is important is because we create dissatisfaction when we create separation.

An obvious example of this is loneliness. Living alone is not the same as feeling lonely. There's no inherent problem about living alone. Yes, it may be preferable to live with a lover or a friend, but there's nothing whatsoever wrong with living alone. There is, on the other hand, a lot wrong with feeling lonely, feeling separated from others. That can be an extremely unpleasant feeling, which can even lead to suicide. Where does loneliness come from? From thoughts! There's no loneliness out there in the world. We create loneliness when we move from Self to self.

Every thought without exception is perspectival, limited, which means that it cannot be the whole truth. The whole truth cannot be thought or spoken. That's logically impossible. The problem is that we are unable to think the whole truth.

There's an obvious solution: return from self to Self. How? Drop thoughts. Do you think sages who may live alone for years in a tiny hut the mountains feel lonely? Not after they wake up to Self. Apprehending the whole truth requires dropping all thoughts because the whole truth is unlimited.

Wisdom is without thought. Practicing wisdom, living well, is usually practicing emptiness, which is being without thought although not, of course, without awareness. The most insidious thoughts are evaluations, judgements that something is good or bad. J. Krishnamurti, the well-known Indian philosopher and spiritual teacher, said, "This is my secret, I don't mind what happens."

Let's take a closer look at the idea of self.

5

❖

The Egoic Mind

There's no difference between mind and the egoic mind. What does that mean? Why is it important?

Here's an initial caution: it's foolish to identify with mind. In other words, you are not your mind. You are not your thoughts. Identifying with mind, identifying with thoughts, is an important mistake that guarantees living poorly. In order to understand why that's the case, let's first consider mind itself.

To have a mind is to be able to think. To mind something is simply to think about it. To think is to have thoughts. Your mind is the whole set or collection of your thoughts.

The phrase 'the egoic mind' is useful in emphasizing **that having a mind is having an ego or self. The ego is the thinker.** Unfortunately, there's no consistent terminology here. To use words as I do, there's no such thing as a thought without a thinker.[36] It's critical to note, however, that *this certainly does not mean that there is no consciousness or awareness without a substantial self who has the awareness.* That's a step way too far.[37]

By any normal criteria, I am a master thinker in the ordinary sense of 'master thinker.' I have a high I.Q. I have a doctorate in philosophy. I think systematically. I'm articulate. I've written dozens of books. I taught at a university for several decades. I made it my goal to become a master thinker and I succeeded.

So?

I also foolishly made the assumption that becoming a master thinker would enable me to be wise, to live well. That's simply false. There's nothing wrong with becoming a master thinker. At least just in terms of making a living, it's important to master something.

However, *mastering thinking is not mastering life*. To identify the two is foolish. I failed to understand that clearly as a young man.

I've just stated the reason: a thinker is an ego. A master thinker is a master ego. Mastering anything requires lots of time and effort. Becoming a master thinker in the ordinary sense of 'master thinker' requires years of the right kind of toil.[38] The more life one spends thinking, the stronger one's ego becomes. Becoming a master thinker requires becoming a powerful ego. Living well requires weakening and dropping the ego, not strengthening it.

Not surprisingly, sages have pointed this out. For example, Osho in <u>Awareness</u>: "The more thoughts you have, the greater the ego you have." For example, Eckhart Tolle in <u>A New Earth</u>: "Ego is always identification with form, seeking yourself and thereby losing yourself in some form . . . More fundamental than the external forms – things and bodies – are the thought forms. . . Whatever you identify with turns into ego."

There are two important consequences to this. First, the more powerful the ego, the more difficult it is to let go of it. So, the better thinker you are, the more difficult it will be for you to awaken. Intellectuals (like me) have a more difficult time waking up. Osho in <u>Intuition</u>: "The more educated a man, the less is the possibility for him to approach the whole."

This becomes an obviously important consequence when combined with the idea of love. Since love requires letting go of ego, the more you have mastered the art of thinking the less easy it will be for you to love.[39]

Second, the more powerful the ego, the more difficult it is to live well. The reason for this is because having a mind or ego is the same as being resistant to reality or what-is. The more powerful the mind or ego, the more resistance there is to reality. **Ego is resistance.** This is important because, since living well requires surrendering to reality (what-is) and, since the more powerful the mind or ego is the more resistance there is to surrendering to reality, the more difficult living well becomes.

In other words, there's also an extraordinary sense of 'master thinker.' It's the sense that someone is a master thinker if and only if one is free to think or not to think. Ordinary people are not free not to think; they are compulsive thinkers. The Buddha says, "a master . . . will think whatever thought he wishes to think and he will not think any thought that he does not wish to think."[40] Remember that thought separates. That is the nature of thought. The **ego is separation**, which is a function of thought.

Ego is absence of the presence of eternity. The death of the ego is the presence of eternity. Ego death opens the temporal to the eternal.

The ego inherently takes itself to be separate. Since everything else is different, it's naturally hostile to everything else. The ego takes itself to be a tiny fragment of a vast, hostile world. It's afraid and sees itself as being in a lonely struggle. Tolle: "The basic ego patterns are designed to combat its own deep-seated fear and sense of lack. They are resistance, control, power, greed, defense, attack. Some of the ego's strategies are extremely clever, yet they never truly solve any of its problems, simply because the ego itself is the problem."[41] How can the ego's problems be solved? Only by the death of the ego. Nothing else suffices. The ego, of course, resists its own demise with every defense it can invent. Because we identify with ego, because we take ourselves to be selves, ego reduction threatens self destruction. **Ego attrition is self attrition. Successful ego attrition is self annihilation.** Whenever we fight ourselves, we find ourselves fighting a very wily opponent indeed. Even though it's false that we are selves, we have identified with being a self for so many years that letting go of that identification is very difficult.

Minor adjustments don't work. Our identification with ego, with thoughts, is much too strong for that. Tinkering around the edges always fails. We are dissatisfied with our lives and turn to various anesthetics to fix our aliments. Some try alcohol or drugs. Others throw themselves into work, sex, video games, sports, or food. Others use television as a numbing device. All these anesthetics and all the others like them fail in terms of living well even though all can be enjoyable when used in moderation. However, when they are used as attempts to soothe the discontent that identification with the egoic mind creates, they not only all fail, but they fail dramatically. When used as anesthetics, they quickly become compulsions or addictions that leave us worse off than before we turned hopefully to them.

Often it takes an important, major loss to realize that we're at a dead-end. Typically, it's only such challenges that force us to admit that our lives are not working well.[42] Once it really sinks in, we realize that *there are only* **two choices***: do whatever it takes to kill the ego or continue to live poorly until death.* Doing whatever it takes requires a major change. As much as we typically dislike having to make minor changes, we typically hate trying to make major changes. However, only a major change will do.

Spiritual teachers have been telling us this for many years. For example, Osho in <u>Awareness</u>: "Unless you bring total effort to waking yourself up, it is not going to happen."

How, though, is it even possible to kill thought, to kill the ego, to kill the egoic mind?

Here's the critical idea: **phenomenological or psychological time sustains the egoic mind**. So, to kill the egoic mind, kill phenomenological time. Stop feeding it. Killing phenomenological or psychological time automatically opens time to eternity. It's not as if that's the first step in some sequence of steps. It's the only step required.

Killing phenomenological time requires *full* awareness of the present moment. Even when we try to focus on it, our everyday awareness of the present moment is almost always only partial. There's "part" of awareness that seems to be running everything in the background. That's the egoic mind.

To kill phenomenological time is to become free from time. To become free from time is to experience eternity. **Living well requires experiencing eternity**.

Once we understand this, it's easy to determine when we are living poorly. There are two clear signs of living poorly. First, whenever we drag our identities from the past into the present moment we are living poorly. That's what we do whenever we drag thoughts into the present moment. Instead of simply being with the sunset, for example, we are judging it, thinking about it.

Second, whenever we look to the future for fulfillment we are living poorly. Whenever we do that we take the present moment to be a stepping stone to a better future, as merely a means to some imagined future end. Bad move. At least when opened to eternity, the present moment is never merely a means to an end. It's whole and infinitely valuable just as it is.

One way to notice this is to admit that the future never arrives. Godot never comes. The future is always only future, which is unreal. Why? If it were to be experienced, it would be real – and also present and, so, not future, not itself.

Huston Smith: "If one's eyes are always on tomorrows, todays slip by unperceived."

Like living poorly, living well happens now. *Now is the time of our lives*. There never is any other time.

To live poorly is to continue to feed the egoic mind. To live well is to live after killing the egoic mind. To practice spiritually or meditatively is to starve the egoic mind with the intention of killing it. Therefore, it's mastering some spiritual or meditative practice that enables us to transition from living poorly to living well.

Such mastering requires learning how to focus fully on the present moment.

What's really going on is that the egoic mind creates phenomenological time, the familiar sense of the passing of time. It's actually a faint but constant mental static. As Tolle puts it in The Power of NOW, it's "an almost continuous low level of unease, discontent, boredom, or nervousness" that is the background music of our ordinary lives. Because it's faint, we may think that it can be easily cured. That's false.

As long as the egoic mind is able to dull, even to a small degree, awareness of the present moment, as long as it's able to obscure, even slightly, awareness of now, it stays alive. Trust me: it really, really wants to stay alive. Killing it 99% of the way doesn't work. Killing it partially fails. It must be totally exterminated.

I emphasize this because our expectations (which, of course, are thoughts) play an important role in how we experience life. If you think that you are going to kill the egoic mind in ten seconds with a single mighty effort, I have bad news for you. It doesn't work like that. In theory, as the Buddha admits, it could happen relatively quickly, for example, in one week.[43] In practice, however, it's never really like that. It took the Buddha himself six years.

There's good news, though, about expectations. Since they are thoughts, dropping thoughts is dropping expectations. It's only *after* we do that that we realize their psychological weight or heaviness. Our lives instantly become lighter and more playful.

Although spontaneous awakenings, in other words, awakenings without deliberately practicing, do occur, without deliberate training they typically fade into memory instead of initiating a new way of living. If so, for life really to improve in a lasting way, what is required is persistent effort of the right kind. If the effort is of the wrong kind, obviously it won't work. You can polish a brick all you want, but it will never reflect like a mirror. However, there are plenty of kinds of methods or techniques that are helpful. Ultimately, though, they, too, need to be dropped. Remember: the effort is not to gain something, but rather to let go of all thought. In that sense, spiritual mastery is not like other kinds of mastery.

What's more important to emphasize here is the persistence of the effort required. Let's drop illusions about that.

In <u>ZEN Merging of East and West</u>, Roshi Kapleau quotes another Zen master about what is required: "To come to full awakening you must act like a man who has fallen into a hundred-foot-deep pit. His thousand, his ten thousand thoughts are reduced to the single thought: 'How can I get out of the pit?' He keeps it up from morning to night and from night to the following morning with no other thought."

Let's suppose that you have understood all this about making an important change in order to kill your egoic mind to live well. What next?

It's simple: begin some classic training and persist.

Of course it's best to investigate the alternatives and select some kind of practice or training for which you are well suited. You may or may not have a background in some spiritual tradition. If you do and it happens to suit you well, perhaps you know an expert who can encourage you to start well. If you lack a spiritual background or yours doesn't suit you well or you don't know a spiritual teacher who is willing to help you, that's not a big deal. You are free to pick and choose. Make a guess about what will work well for you and go for it. If you are lucky, you'll find one on your first or second try.[44] If you are less lucky, no matter: keep checking out different kinds until you find one you are able to commit to wholeheartedly.[45]

I warn you against trying to invent your own or combining different practices. Why? There are classic practices that have been working for hundreds or thousands of years. They've already been perfected. Use what's ready-to-hand. Unless you are a spiritual genius, you'll fail. Emulate the successful who have already blazed the trail. Success has left clues for us to follow.

Once you begin, just follow instructions. If reading helps you to practice, read; if reading doesn't help you to practice, stop reading.

The idea is to stop doing and just be. The Buddha was correct in distinguishing "three kinds of action . . . bodily action, verbal action, and mental action."[46] Thinking is mental action. The Buddha continues, "I describe mental action as the most reprehensible for the performance of evil action." Thinking is the chief cause of wrong acts. Why? Thinking separates and wrong acts are always grounded on separation. *Practicing letting go of thinking automatically undermines immoral behavior.* "Meditate, bhikkus, do not delay or else you will regret it later. This is our instruction to you."[47]

You will have questions, questions about practicing and not just theoretical questions. It's really helpful if you have a master who works with you and knows you to answer your questions.[48]

Especially at first, however, you may not be in that position. Permit me to warn you against something that will likely keep obstructing your progress.

Yes, progress. Despite just claiming that the egoic mind must be killed in order to live well, it's not all or nothing. Spiritual training wounds the ego before killing it. Furthermore, it's important to understand why it's not all or nothing, why it's not either/or. Let's turn to that topic next.

6

❖

The Spiritual Materialism Trap

Again, words and concepts are never quite right. For example, although doing so is not unusual, talking about life on the spiritual way as a 'training' or 'practice' is somewhat misleading. Please keep in mind that, like being a genuine philosopher, it's an unusual, extraordinary way of living.

A major problem of that way of living is called "spiritual materialism." Despite the possibility that the bodymind is one, it nevertheless seems that what is material is not the same as what is mental. "Materialism" is an ontological doctrine that claims that to be real is to be material. Materialists "reduce" what appears to be nonmaterial (such as consciousness) to matter and its states. By contrast, "spiritualism" is an ontological doctrine that claims that to be real is to be spiritual. Spiritualists "reduce" what appears to be nonspiritual (such as physical objects) to the mental and its states. A chief difficulty with either of these positions is making clear the key concepts of matter and spirit, which, despite not having a clear nature, do seem antithetical.

It automatically follows from this that "spiritual materialism" is also unclear. It may nevertheless prove a useful concept for us to consider.

We've considered how the ego separates me from what isn't me. That idea is what is behind our use of words such as 'I,' 'me,' and 'mine.' Letting go of ego, detaching from the concept of self, is what the spiritual way of life is all about. Its purpose is to reduce egocentricity until the ego is dead.

The Buddha repeatedly stresses this. For example, he says to his son, "all material form should be seen as it actually is with proper wisdom thus: 'this is not mine, this I am not, this is not my self.'"[49] Similarly, "Form, feeling, and perception, / Consciousness, and formations -- / 'I am not this, this isn't mine,' / Thus one is detached from it.'[50] Similarly, a sage "sees all form as it really is with correct wisdom thus: 'This is not mine, this I am not, this is not my self.'"[51]

Spiritual materialism is the doctrine the ego uses in order to get you to stop attacking it. Anyone who has ever seriously attempted ego attrition quickly realizes that the ego is a very clever opponent. Its opposition comes in various ways. Those ways are called "spiritual materialism." They are spiritual traps.

An important such trap is the all-or-nothing argument. This is the either/or thought made popular by Kierkegaard. If my living the spiritual way (my practicing, my training) has not yet caused me to wake up, then it must be useless. I've tried hard and failed, so I might as well quit. If the ego can get you to accept or attach to that thought, it wins. Your attempts at ego attrition are over. (The better way to think is that, if you are working on your practice, your practice is working on you whether you realize it or not. As the Buddha remarks "Little by little a person becomes good, as a water pot is filled by drops of water."[52])

Another such trap is the perfectionist trap: if my living the spiritual way hasn't yet succeeded despite my best efforts, I must be doing something wrong. My technique must somehow be faulty. At least until I can understand what I'm doing wrong, I might as well stop trying. Again, if the ego can get you to accept that argument, it wins. (The better way to think is that, if you are simply following classic instructions, your technique is fine.)

Another such trap is the comparison trap: I've been practicing longer than S [someone else] and yet S has awakened and I haven't. Therefore, I must be doing something wrong. Perhaps I'm not well-suited to waking up. So I should stop trying. Again, if the ego can get you to accept that agument, it wins. (The better way to think, since it is just more thinking, is simply to drop comparing yourself to others.)

All such traps are based on a common assumption that is false. That common assumption is the thought that living the spiritual way is supposed to produce a beneficial result for you. The practitioner or trainee is supposed eventually to gain something important, namely, a breakthrough to a state of grace full of abiding joy, lasting peace, and genuine love.

What's wrong with that? After all, isn't awakening and then leading an awakened life the goal of living the spiritual way?

If you think it is, *you are thinking* that it is. That means, obviously, that you are thinking. So <u>thinking is a necessary condition of spiritual materialism</u>.

However, **not-thinking is all that is required for waking up**. To wake up, even for a moment, is to let go of *all* thoughts.

So as long as you remain stuck thinking that the purpose of living the spiritual way is awakening, attachment to that thought itself will prevent detachment from thought. It's impossible simultaneously to be attached to thought and detached from thought.

Another way to think about this is to admit that the ego is essentially characterized by greediness or acquisitiveness. It's never satisfied for more than an instant with what it has; it always wants more and more and more. It's perpetually restless. It constantly flees the present moment. It's never at peace; it's always at war.

The ego wants you to try to gain something from living the spiritual way. Why? As long as you are trying to gain something, you'll fail. As long as you fail, the ego will continue to live. Furthermore, the ego is perfectly familiar with living to gain, which is what it does incessantly.

This explains why sages, who are awake and living well, have been warning against spiritual materialism at least since the time of the historical Buddha some 2400 years ago.

You should be skeptical of every claim I make. I'm no sage. I'm just an old philosopher who has, though, been attempting to live the spiritual way for decades. So, again, permit me to quote a few sages as social proof before explaining why the whole idea of a sage is dubious. Since I'm most familiar with them, I'll quote from the Buddha and from the Zen tradition, but that really makes little difference.

Speaking of identifying with the body, the Buddha says, "There can be no considering that as 'I' or 'mine' or 'I am.'"[53] It's critical to detach from identification with any form including bodily form.

Kosho Uchiyama: "You can't practice true zazen if your practice is for the sake of seeing positive results . . . It is a big mistake to think that the practice will open up in you a special state of mind or a unique environment . . . there isn't any special state of mind."

Kobun Chino, Roshi: "One must disappear in the sitting [practicing]; that is the only way . . ." If you disappear as a separate person, then you won't be enjoying any special benefits.

The best illustration in the Zen tradition comes from The Heart Sutra. The Heart of Perfect Wisdom [Prajna Paramita Hridaya] is chanted daily by Zen practitioners (trainees, students). "Form is emptiness; emptiness also is form. Emptiness is no other than form; form is no other than emptiness. In the same way, feeling, discrimination, formation, and consciousness are emptiness."[54] Similarly, "all phenomena are emptiness, without characteristics, without arising, without ceasing." In fact, there is "no [spiritual] path, no wisdom, no attainment, and no nonattainment."[55]

Obviously, if there's no wisdom, it's impossible to become wise. **Wisdom is emptiness.**

Remember the context here: the ego wants you to be guilty of spiritual materialism. It wants you to try to gain something from walking the spiritual path, from living the spiritual way. Why? As long as you are trying to gain something for yourself, you are being egocentric. As long as you are being egocentric, the ego will continue to live.

It really helps to let these ideas sink in. If there is no wisdom, if there is nothing to attain, then why would you try to attain something? If wisdom really is emptiness, how could it possibly be attained?

Living well, being wise, requires nonresistance, acceptance, allowing, surrendering to the present moment. Why?

The only alternative is resistance to the present moment, which is what trying to gain something is. Since the present moment already is what it is, resistance is inevitably nothing but fruitless rebellion.

It's important to understand that it's not necessary to like the present moment. Had you been given a choice, what's real right now may well not have been something you'd have chosen. It's possible to allow it to be just as it is without liking it.

Nonresistance is nothing but fully accepting the reality of the present moment. It's just letting it be as it already is. It's wholly accepting life as it is right now.

Obviously, nonresistance cannot change anything about what-is. Nothing can change what-is. However, it can permanently improve everything about the quality of your life.

Allowing the present moment to be includes letting go of all thoughts about the past and the future. It also includes letting go of all thoughts about elsewhere.

From now on, please watch for your own patterns of resistance. There are two major patterns.

First, suppose that you have suffered a serious loss and you yearn for reality to be as it used to be in the past. You desire that there be no gap between the reality of the present moment and (your thoughts about) how reality used to be. By attending to that gap and paying homage to it, you are (almost certainly without intending to do so) creating your own suffering. To dissolve that suffering, adopt the attitude of simply allowing the present moment to be just as it is. If it helps, you can even imagine yourself choosing it to be just as it is by thinking that life is using it to try to teach you an important, though difficult, lesson.

Second, suppose that you dislike your present situation and yearn for a different situation in the future. By attending to the gap between what-is and how you would like it to be, you are creating your own suffering. To dissolve it, adopt an attitude of nonresistance to what-is right here, right now.

This partially explains why living well, mastering the spiritual way of life, is initially so difficult. It's like bodybuilders who pursue two incompatible goals simultaneously. On the one hand, they want to gain muscle; on the other hand, they want to lose fat. It's not that difficult to increase muscle and fat simultaneously, and it's not that difficult to decrease muscle and fat simultaneously. It's very difficult to achieve both goals simultaneously. Similarly, in a spiritual practice such as zazen, we are simultaneously trying to relax into rather than to resist what-is while intensely trying to awaken. That seems impossible. Striving and relaxing are contradictory.

The solution is let go of conceptual striving and to strive instead with one's gut. Roshi Kapleau writes in The Three Pillars of Zen that "to strive self-consciously for satori or any other gain from zazen is as unnecessary as it is undesirable." This doesn't mean to stop striving, in other words, practicing intensely. As he quotes Ju-ching as saying, "You must exert yourselves with all your might. . ." Exerting yourself in this way does not mean thinking furiously. It means bringing focus back to here and now whenever you notice that a thought has arisen. As Roshi Kapleau says and any long-time practitioner can confirm, it requires "an intense inner struggle" against the power of the discursive intellect, the conceptualizing mind.

As Roshi Kapleau quotes Dogen: mastery "involves the highest form of exertion, which goes on unceasingly . . . It is sustained exertion . . . This sustained exertion is not something which men of the world naturally love or desire, yet it is the last refuge of all."

One advantage of the Zen tradition is koan training. A koan is a spiritual knot that cannot be untied by the intellect. Koans cause intellectual distress and cannot be passed conceptually. Conceptually, they are simple. Roshi Kapleau gives us the secret: "the import of every koan is the same: that the world is one interdependent Whole and that each separate one of us is that Whole." (That's why you are infinitely valuable.) Merely thinking that thought, however, is not realization.

No thought is the key to living well. Why? Waking up cannot be conceptualized. It cannot be thought or understood. It can only be experienced directly. Yasutani Roshi urges: "Cease clinging to all thought-forms! I stress this because it is the central point of Zen practice."[56] The key insight with respect to living well and purpose is that **dissatisfaction requires time**. No time, no dissatisfaction. There is never any suffering in the present moment. What? Isn't, for example, a broken bone distress? No, it's a broken bone. Isn't heartbreak loneliness? No, it's thought of separation. There may be a present situation that you don't like, but all situations are acceptable. Unless the egoic mind turns a momentary situation into a problem with a temporal duration, it's impossible to be dissatisfied. There are no problems whatsoever in the present moment. Why? Problems require temporal duration.

It's good to be skeptical about this, but please don't be negative. Try to think of a counter-example. Suppose that right now you have painful cramps or diarrhea. Well, that's an unpleasant situation. Accept it fully. If there's something you can do to alleviate your discontent, do it. If not, just let all resistance go.

In other words, being in that situation is not being ill. An illness is temporal; it has a beginning, middle, and end. Illness requires time. If you permit the egoic mind to label your present situation as illness, you have transformed the present situation into an illness. Instead of just having painful cramps or diarrhea, you now are suffering from an illness. Now you are sick.

The egoic mind is the wellspring of resistance. That's why it's important to kill the egoic mind if you want to live well.

Insofar as we focus on the future or on the past, we are thinking. We are trapping ourselves in thoughts. We are reinforcing the egoic mind.

The right way of focusing is to focus only on the present moment. This blocks becoming lost in thoughts about the past or the future. This focusing is not thinking; instead, it's just non-conceptual awareness. To emphasize the difference, it's often called "witnessing" or "watching" or "observing" rather than thinking or conceptualizing.

Incidentally, please don't draw the conclusion from this that, for example, you should somehow try to cut off everything related to the past and the future. That would be idiotic. Suppose, for example, that you reject attending your 20th or 50th high school reunion because it's all "past stuff." Don't be silly! Instead, attend the reunion mindfully and reconnect with classmates from yesteryear. Why? In a sense, rejecting them would be rejecting part of your own life. As I explain in what follows, there's no real separation between them and you. Similarly, it would be idiotic not occasionally to plan for the future. If you and I are meeting for lunch tomorrow, we'd better set a time to meet as well as a place.

Our most fundamental freedom is freedom of focus. We are able to focus on whatever we want. The more we focus on something, the more important it becomes. Combining three of the Buddha's ideas about this is helpful. First, "What one thinks about, that one mentally proliferates."[57] That's simply a fact about how we think. When focus on something, we tend to think more and more about it. Second, when we focus on conditioned forms, "there is mind affected by lust, by hate, and by delusion. Unwholesome habits originate from this."[58] All temporal forms are conditioned. As we think about forms we don't identify with, we naturally desire some, get upset about others, and are blinded by others. This creates dissatisfaction. Third, "all conditioned things are of a nature to decay."[59] All forms are impermanent. Why not cease focusing on conditioned forms? In other words, why not drop thinking if only to see whether our lives get better or not? Why not focus on emptiness, the unconditioned, by dropping all thoughts about forms? That's what practicing does. Practice well and find out for yourself whether or not your dissatisfaction diminishes.

I think of focusing well as simply relying on our brains. Usually, our brains work fine, which is why it's wise simply to trust them. Do exactly that in dangerous situations that require immediate action. Thinking is hardly immediate. In fact, it's not only very slow but it also hurts, which explains why we tend to rely on habits rather than on doing much of it. Our brains are typically able to notice forms and react appropriately whenever spontaneous action is required.

Avoid thinking that waking up (superconsciousness, <u>samadhi</u>) results in apprehending a brown mix of indistinguishable objects. Instead, it results in the clarity and freshness of nonconceptual apprehension. Without concepts to deaden experience, the world becomes more alive and sparkling. As

Eckhart Tolle writes in <u>The Power of NOW</u>, being fully awake is our "natural state of *felt* oneness with Being."

Killing the egoic mind does not mean that sages have killed their ability to think. Not at all. In fact, that ability seems to strengthen when it isn't continuously utilized.

There's no doubt that these ideas are difficult to grasp. Why? It's really because you think of yourself as something. As soon as you drop that idea, these ideas will instantly make a lot more sense. Let's try an analogy that may help letting go.

7

❖

You as Tornado

Reificationism is a sin best minimized. It may also be the important sin that is least familiar to you. It occurs whenever we take dynamic processes to be static forms. The noun is derived from the verb '(to) reify.'

Its deepest and most insidious occurrence is when we reify ourselves, our selves.

A way to warm up to this idea is to ask yourself: is anything natural static?

Think of stars, clouds, lakes, weather, trees, mountains, animals, rain, or any other naturally occurring forms. Aren't they all in incessant flux? If you look closely enough, you can "see" that even a stone is not as unchanging as it initially appears.

In The Heart of Understanding, Thich Nhat Hanh closely examines just a piece of paper and argues that all such physical forms "inter-are" with every other entity.

Scientists tell us that physical forms are made of molecules that are made of atoms that are something like tiny solar systems. Apprehended this way, the natural world appears as ceaseless, living movement. It's a perpetual flux.

Is the world *you* inhabit mostly dead or mostly alive?

It's likely mostly dead. In fact, instead of death, it's life itself that typically requires explanation in the modern world, which is essentially understood as being like a machine rather than an organism. How did life ever arise from non-life? If your world is mostly dead, that's because you don't live in the real world; instead, you mostly live in thoughts.

Although they can be changed, concepts are static. They are lifeless. They are also the critical constituents of all thoughts or judgments. No concepts, no thoughts.

The more you live in your thoughts, the more your experiences will be stale, dull, or boring. Done that. Been there. Next? Let's have something fresh instead. That's the world of a bored teenager hanging out with nothing to do.

The more life you live in your thoughts instead of in the world, the more you are likely to feel that life has lost its freshness, sparkle, and vitality. Experiences become more and more jaded.

That's the inevitable result of reificationism.

Please challenge yourself by asking: How have I fallen into the dreadful habit of reificationism?

The good news is that it has a cause. It doesn't just happen. If we are able to understand how it happens, perhaps we can unbind our lives.

Here's an important clue: some thinkers call reificationism "nominalization." A nomen in Latin is a name. A name is a bit of language used to refer to forms.

Apparently, de-nominalization is an important strategy in neuro-linguistic programming. For example, Richard Bandler argues that "*change happens constantly, and easily, and making it work for you is a matter of understanding how to run your own brain.*"[60] If NLP practitioners are right, it's wise to avoid reificationism.

If we let 'conscious' denote 'the content of awareness in the present moment' and 'unconscious' denote 'everything except what is conscious,' the problem with using our brains more effectively is that they are dominated by unconscious processes. Richard Bandler and John Grinder in Frogs Into Princes: "it's the unconscious processes and parts of the person you've *got* to work with effectively in order to bring about change in an efficient way."

This isn't mere theory. Failing to understand how unconscious brain processes work dooms attempts to improve the quality of life to being, at best, inefficient and, at worst, ineffective.

A common example is that brain processes don't "get" negativity. Therefore, if you are trying to reduce your percentage of body fat and keep telling yourself "Do *not* eat the chocolate cake in the refrigerator," what you are actually doing is training your brain to eat the chocolate cake in the refrigerator. Simply understanding the sentence 'Do not eat the chocolate cake in the refrigerator' requires thinking about that desirable cake.

In fact, initially just thinking "I am fat and should become less fat" already identifies you with being fat. This is a good example of reificationism at work: you take yourself to be a separate object with a certain property. That just reinforces your self-image, your conception of yourself as fat.

The whole process of conceptualizing requires fabrication. *Reificationism is based on the delusion that processes are things.* Except for concepts and thoughts, nothing temporal is static. Everything temporal is in flux. Everything temporal is a process.

The Buddha's most original and perhaps most profound point, that there are no separate selves, may be understood as an attempt to undermine reificationism. He wanted and urged us to open up to the natural flow of the world without attaching to conceptualizations or nominalizations. (This may explain why he never wrote any books, namely, to avoid providing us with more static objects to attach to.)

In The Spell of the Sensuous David Abram argues that it was the development of writing systems that finally cut our ties "to the mysteries of a more-than-human world." This explains why the natural, non-human world no longer seems to us alive. It no longer speaks to us, whereas 'In indigenous, oral cultures, nature itself is articulate; it *speaks*." The less the world talks to us, the more alienated, isolated, and separated we feel.

It doesn't follow that the development of writing systems was bad. They have given us important benefits. However, there's no free lunch. Like the benefits of the first and second agricultural revolutions, we have paid a high price for those benefits and we seldom pause to realize how much we have paid for them.

It's sufficient to consider our ordinary temporal concepts to obtain at least a faint sense of what reificationism continues to cost us. Instead of taking for granted that the future and past are "autonomous realms existing apart from the sensuous present," it is possible to rediscover them "as aspects of the corporeal present," in other words, to locate them in the sensuous, other-than-human processes all around us.

To begin to grasp the importance of this, please ask yourself: "Apart from future and past, who am I?"

If you let it, your autobiography, your self story, the ongoing narrative of which you are the protagonist, will begin to unravel. Ask: "**In the present moment, who am I?**"

Having trouble answering? What does "I" stand for in the present moment?

After all, if the world is made of stories and stories require time, then stories are inapplicable in the present moment. What are we when emptied of our stories? This is troubling because stories are our default way of understanding.

Reificationism is at its most insidious when autologously applied.

Consider this idea seriously: you are eternal emptiness.

To be a human being is to be like a tornado or cyclone.

We come to understand new forms by comparing them to forms we already understand. This is why it's very often helpful to ask about something new "What is it like?" rather than "What is it?" It's by noticing the similarities and differences among forms that we increase our conceptual understanding of them.

How do you understand yourself? That's an important question.

At least since the days of Aristotle (384 B.C. to 322 B.C.) in the west, the dominant analogy, suitably updated, is to a pin cushion.[61] We are substrata in which qualities inhere much in the way that pins stick in a pin cushion. You, for example, are not merely a set or list of qualities; instead, you are a cluster of qualities held together by something. Suppose, say, that you go on a reducing diet and go from weighing 180 pounds to 160 pounds. When you undergo any sort of qualitative change, it's like removing one pin and replacing it with another pin. So take out the pin that stands for 180 pounds and replace it with the pin that stand for 160 pounds. When you undergo change of location such as when you walk a mile down the road, that's simply moving the pin cushion with all its pins a mile down the road. In other words, despite any such change of qualities or location, you remain the same person through time.

This analogy may have been originated, and is certainly enhanced, by the structure of language. To judge that you weigh 160 pounds is to think that there is a subject, you, who has a certain predicate or quality, weighing 160 pounds. That quality isn't just floating out there in the world; instead, it's had by something.

For whatever reason, it's quite natural for a westerner like me to go through life thinking that I am something. What kind am I? I'm a substantial continuant [something that is literally the same at two or more consecutive times] from birth until death. Who am I? I'm a particular continuant with a specific set of qualities.

There is, however, a simple, fundamental problem with this analogy. What is the substance itself? What's the substratum? What's the pin cushion? After all, it's possible to perceive a pin cushion because it has familiar qualities such as shape, color, texture, weight, and so on. That's where the analogy breaks down. According to it, you are like a pin cushion despite the fact that, unlike a pin cushion, your substratum itself has no qualities. It's of the essence to realize that the qualities of an individual are represented in the analogy by the pins, not by the pin cushion itself.[62] It's impossible to single out a qualityless form.

Two questions remain unanswered. What kind am I? Who am I?

Those are serious questions. If you have never seriously asked them, please start.

Let's try a wholly different analogy. Try thinking of yourself as being like a tornado.[63] What is a tornado? It's a weather vortex in which stuff whirls around an empty center. Here, your qualities are that stuff.

If so, your center is nothing at all; instead, it's an emptiness. There's ultimately no "you" to single out; there's no person inside somewhere. You are nothing but a conglomeration of qualities temporarily whirling around an empty center. That explains why there's no inner substratum to single out. There is no central "I" in there at all.

Despite the fact that the Zen tradition has produced some marvelous writings, transmission outside such writings has always been a critical theme in the history of Zen. It's good to have such writings, such fossilized concepts and judgments, to guide us, but it's better to use them and then discard them rather than to attach to them.

Where's any requirement for literacy? Some Zen masters have, in fact, been illiterate. Since attachment to the written word fosters reificationism, it obstructs awakening. (This explains why intellectuals, thought mongerers like me, usually take longer to wake up.)

I've read that the most commonly used words are 'I' and 'me" and presumably also their cognates such as 'my' and 'mine.' Whenever we use them, we are committing the sin of reificationism, which is a way of deceiving ourselves.

This is actually good news. You are much more than you ordinarily think you are. Your eternal emptiness is what prevents your separation from everything else. **Conceptualizing separates; emptiness unites**. Our central emptiness is a blessing rather than a curse.

Does the tornado analogy seem far-fetched? It's not. Here's a simple test that may help. Please take it. It's important.

Describe your favorite room. If you don't have a favorite room, describe a room that you know very well. Imagine that you are a novelist and that that room features prominently in your story. That's it. Stop reading for a few moments and imagine that room in detail. Describe it to yourself.

Did you do it? No cheating!

Alright. Now please think about your description. Did you describe the room's walls, ceiling and floor? Did you describe the furniture in the room? Probably. Is there anything important missing from your description of that room?

If you are like most people, there is something important missing. What?

The room itself! The space. The emptiness that is bounded by the walls, ceiling, and floor and partially filled up by the furniture. Did you describe that emptiness? Really?

As Buddhists think and talk, a "form" is anything we can single out for our attention (whether in perception, imagination, or conception). It doesn't even really matter whether or not it is real, or whether it is taken to be real. For example, a dream object is a form. Any qualitied particular is a form.

"Emptiness" is anything that may contain forms; unlike forms, it's not an individual that can be singled out.

The walls, ceiling, floor, and furniture of your room are forms, whereas the space itself is emptiness.

The fact is that *we tend to focus our attention on forms*. When someone asks you what you see when you look into the heavens on a dark, clear night, you'll likely reply, "Stars." Stars are forms. Stars have qualities, and all qualities are forms. Of course, if there weren't also emptiness or void in which the stars are located, you wouldn't see individual stars at all.

Everything we encounter in our everyday lives may be conceptualized as either emptiness or form.

We ourselves are somehow a combination of forms and emptiness. Thinking hard about our own natures can produce a headache. The reason is because, at least if you are like me in this respect, our tendency is to keep trying to introspect some inner self or person. As the Buddha first pointed out and, in the west, as Hume also pointed out, using introspection to find that inner self always fails to yield one.

Why not let go of the idea that you are a person? Why not accept the idea that your core is only emptiness?

Try this: you are not a self or person having experiences. Instead, you are a set of experiences, a process. Ultimately you are empty. Osho in Intuition: "what I mean by 'empty' – at leisure, relaxed, nontense, not moving, not desiring, not going anywhere, just being here, utterly here." Realizing this is what a spiritual practice is about: "relaxation is the basis of meditation." **Meditation is living no-thought**. Why meditate? "You only *are* whenever you stop thinking."

Zen master Bassui emphasizes that you are Void (Mind with a capital 'm,' buddha-nature) rather than being a person: "your own Mind is itself Buddha, the Void-universe. There will then be no anxiety about life or death, no truth to search for . . . keep your mind as empty as space."[64]

This is why Zen master Rinzai says, "There is nothing in particular to realize."[65] What's essential is just getting rid all notions (thoughts, concepts. ideas) including those of buddha-nature and self. "The essential thing for enlightenment is to empty the mind . . ."

Harada-roshi: "Self-realization is not a matter of step-by-step progress but the result of a leap. Until your mind is pure you cannot make this leap."[66] A pure mind is a mind empty of all thoughts.

This undermines the idea that we are going to work on ourselves and slowly become better and better. No. There's no self to improve. *Self-improvement is a delusion.* Eckhart Tolle: "You do not become good by trying to be good, but by finding the goodness that is already within you . . . But it can only emerge if something fundamental changes in your state of consciousness . . . how 'spiritual' you are has nothing to do with what you believe but everything to do with your state of consciousness."[67] The state of consciousness required is one without ego or any other temporal concepts, in other words, awareness of the eternal at this moment. "This is why we may also call it Presence. The ultimate purpose of human existence . . . is to bring that power into this world." Of course, we "can only be present Now."

Although it's convenient to do so, this is why it's misleading to talk about sages. There aren't any! There are no awakened persons for the simple reason that there are no persons. **Nothing is personal.**

So, however convenient it is, it's actually better to drop the idea that persons are awake or asleep. Instead, think in terms of experiences. Specifically, think in terms of optimal experiences, which are free and unconditioned. An optimal experience is a selfless experience. It's often called a moment of Zen. Instead of thinking of yourself as a person having an optimal experience, if you have ever had one you realize that you are nothing but the experience itself. In other words, there's nothing separating you from the experiencing.

Think of some skill that you have learned. Walking. Reading. Driving. Shooting a jump shot in basketball. Dancing. Riding a bicycle. Firing a slap shot in hockey. It doesn't matter. At first, you had to think about what you were doing. Eventually, with sufficient practice, "it" just happened. Instead of trying to dance, you were the dancing.[68] Those episodes were episodes of living well. They were not only selfless, but also notice that they were without time consciousness. Phenomenological time disappears during optimal experiences. In other words, although you might be able later to figure out how long they lasted, during them, you are not conscious of the passing of time. You are also not conscious of a self having them. Notice that those experiences, which can occasionally occur quite spontaneously, are not only natural but are joyful as well as wholly satisfying. There's no dissatisfaction when living well.

Sengcan: "Awakening is to go beyond / both emptiness and form."

What? What does that mean? How are we to understand waking up?

It's easier to understand awakened experiences than awakened persons. Again, there are no persons if by 'persons' we are referring to selves, continuant substrata. If you insist, if it's a step too far to drop the concept of a person, think instead of a sage, an awakened person, simply as a string of awakened experiences, which are optimal experiences.

There really is no understanding waking up. To understand is to conceptualize and to wake up is to stop conceptualizing. "This ultimate finality . . . can't be described."[69] Why? To describe it would be to conceptualize it. Rather than thought, direct experience is required to apprehend it.

Here's the key: "In this true world of Emptiness, both self and other are no more."[70] In other words, it's beyond ego death.

There's no separation between, say, me and you. *To have an ego is to have a self-concept.* To have a self-concept is to be able to sort objects into self and not self. *What happens if we drop our self-concepts? We automatically stop separating ourselves from everything else.*

Remember that separation is always the cause of dissatisfaction. What happens when we stop separating ourselves from everything else? Dissatisfaction disappears.

The separation doesn't just apply to separating ourselves from other people. It applies to separating ourselves from all other forms. "To enter this true empty world, immediately affirm 'not-two.'"[71] In other words, to wake up is to drop the idea of being separate from everything else.

If, as is likely, you've had an occasional optimal experience, you already have experienced the lack of separation that comes from any experience uncontaminated by thought. In other words, you've already experienced no-thought (or no-mind); you've already tasted living well.

If, then, you are not a self in the sense of being a continuant substratum, with what should you identify? Let's answer that question.

8

❖

Your Being

Time is meaningless in eternity. So if you wholly identify with anything temporal, you're thinking of your life as meaningless. The more thoroughly you identify with anything temporal, the more you are thinking of your life as being without primary purpose.

What do most of us identify with?

With what is temporal and taken to be us, namely, our bodies and our thoughts. We think of our bodies as having a life span of so many decades. We think of our thoughts as accompanying our aging bodies. We think of ourselves in terms of the stories of our lives, our autobiographies.

Stories are temporal. There's no such thing as a momentary story. *By accepting and attaching to our stories or to anything else that's temporal, we are sowing the seeds of our own dissatisfaction.* That's not just foolish, it's madness.

What is mad is limiting ourselves to our doings. What are our doings? The sum total of what we think, say, or do (in the sense of our behaviors). The implicit judgment is that it's what we do that matters.

No, it's not. It's not that it doesn't matter at all. It's not that we lack a history of thinking, speaking, and doing. It's not that thinking that way is useless. It's that it's misleading because it's radically incomplete. It ignores our center or essence in favor of what is peripheral.

In terms of the tornado, it's like focusing on all the stuff whirling around the periphery and ignoring the empty, still center that is the heart of the tornado.

Our center or *essence is eternity*. We are emptiness, which is peacefulness. We are unable to pass Pascal's test, we are unable to be at ease, because we have identified solely with what we *do* and completely ignored what we *are*. <u>We are human beings; we are not merely human doings.</u>

This misidentification is the cause of all our sorrows. It is this ignorance that explains the common human madness, our shared insanity.

Actually, I've watered this down to make it more palatable. The truth is that there's no difference between being and awakened doing. In other words, "Without an awareness of being, there can be no truly meaningful doing. Any doing that lacks awareness of the being aspect becomes a frenzied thing, a do-gooding, that will often do more harm than good."[72] Similarly, John Daido Loori writes, "The presence of self, the subtlest hint of self-centeredness, creates the difference between a 'do-gooder' and the manifestation of true compassion."[73] The task is to avoid being a "do-gooder" by waking up in order to live true compassion.

The reality is that time and eternity contradict each other. If so, how could both be real?

If one must be unreal, is it time or eternity that is unreal?

If you value freedom from all temporal tribulations, it's better that it's eternity that is real rather than temporality. Could the center of the tornado exist apart from all the whirling debris around its circumference? Yes.

You now have license to identify with the eternal rather than with the temporal.

Why do we still tend to fear dying or being dead? Why are we still tempted to identify with what we *do* rather than with what we *are*?

It really comes from the habit of living in our thoughts, which is what we do whenever we think. We exercise the egoic mind so constantly that it now seems natural that we are egos. It's this incessant exercise that obscures our true nature, which is what we really are. In other words, we have lost perspective on ourselves.

Our egos are never satisfied for more than a moment. They always crave more and more and more. Most of us spend our lives feeding them. Why? We think that our well-being (happiness) comes from the situations we find ourselves in. That explains why we spend most of our waking lives trying to improve our situations. However, it's false that our well-being comes from our situations; instead, it comes from our interpretations of our situations. Therefore, fortunately, we don't have to change the world to be happy. We only have to change our interpretations of our situations, which is what all the wise do and all the foolish fail to do. Some of us question the wisdom of continually trying to change the world. Some, the wise, set themselves free.

You can emulate the wise or not. If you don't know anyone who is wise, and you may not, at least you can read books by and about them. There's no better social proof than that.

You've probably encountered Einstein's often quoted remark that "Problems cannot be solved by the same level of thinking that created them."

You may not, however, have encountered Tolle's follow-up: "The problems of the mind cannot be solved on the level of the mind."

Even if you have heard of Ramana Maharshi, you may never have heard of his simple claim that "The mind is <u>maya</u>." 'Maya' is a Sanskrit word that here refers to the veil of illusion that takes all forms to be in groundless, ceaseless flux. All temporal forms are in flux. Even stars and galaxies die. However, no form is groundless. Each form, including each human form, has an essence of emptiness or eternality.

There's nothing wrong with appreciating temporal forms. Of course we should appreciate a sunset or a flower or a tiger or another human.

Where we go wrong is in clinging to them, trying to attach ourselves to the impermanent. *The central error comes from the fact that we have to discriminate to cling.* Instead of understanding the equal value of all forms, we set some up as sacred, which is a way of living poorly. *Instead, appreciate all forms as sacred and cling to none of them.* That's the way to living well.

Sengcan: "If mind does not discriminate, all things are as they are, as One . . . one thing is all, all things are one."

That's how *we get upside-down with respect to life's purpose.*

We've considered the distinction between our primary purpose and our secondary purposes in Chapter 1. I'm using 'upside-down' here as it's used in real estate. Suppose that you have a mortgage on your house. You are upside-down with respect to that mortgage if you owe whoever holds the mortgage more money than your house is worth.

With respect to our primary and secondary purposes, you are upside-down if you think that your secondary purposes are more important than your primary purpose. That means that you are thoroughly confused about what makes your life important or meaningful. Why? Secondary purposes are always accidental, whereas our primary purpose is essential to our human being.

It may help to loosen your attachment to your secondary purposes to ask the purpose question of other beings. What is the purpose of a rock? What is the purpose of a flower? What is the purpose of a tiger? Do they even have purposes?

It may help to loosen your attachment to your secondary purposes to imagine the following: suppose that you were condemned to live the rest of your life alone on a desert island.

Would that undermine any possibility of a meaningful life? Would that eliminate the possibility that your life would have a purpose?

I ask this because our secondary purposes are often tightly bound up with other people. We identify with our secondary purposes. I am a mother. I am a teacher. I am a daughter. I am a friend. And so on.

Well, you may be all those things. You may have all those secondary purposes. There's nothing wrong with any of them or with any similar ones. Question: if, for whatever reason, you lost all those roles, would you still be you? Isn't it very odd to think that you wouldn't be you?

However closely you tend to identify with it, *none of your secondary purposes is essential to your being you.* So none of them is your purpose as a human being. Your purpose as a human being is to be a human being. It is not merely to engage in a set of human doings.

It's impossible to be a human being without opening to eternity, which is the stillness of being itself. A human life that is closed to eternity is not a fully human life.

In other words, we are more than protagonists in our own stories. In fact, we are infinitely more than that. Our value as human beings is infinite. Our purpose is to open to eternity, to open the temporal to the eternal. We are of cosmic importance.

As human beings whose essence is eternity, our work is to open time to eternity. How important are you? Think of yourself as like a chick in an egg trying to break free except that you are trying to break free from time in order to free all other beings as well.

Incidentally, other beings can sense this. You may already understand that if you live with a pet such as a dog or a cat. For example, if you happen to be practicing near such a pet, you may notice that they approach and settle near you as if to be in your aura. That's happened to me with both cats and dogs that were not even my pets. It's a sign that the world appreciates our spiritual efforts, that we are important to the world. By way of contrast, other animals are often afraid of strange humans because those animals sense the madness of most humans.

The way to grasp this idea of essence conceptually is to disconnect your life from time. Have you ever lived outside the present moment? Have you ever lived now in the past or in the future? No, of course not.

So set aside the past and the future. *What is the primary purpose of your life right now?* What is the primary purpose of your life in this present instant? What are you now?

Oops. All stories just disappeared. Why? Again, stories take time. Since time is what the present moment lacks, we just released all stories.

So answer: What is the primary purpose of your life right now?

It's to be wholly what you are right here and now. What's that? *A temporal being open to eternity. You are essentially what you are in the present moment.*

You may not realize it, but that's what your purpose is. If you fail to realize it, you are out of alignment with reality. If you realize it, you are in alignment with reality. Since peacefulness comes from being, if you want to be peaceful, just stop thinking and you'll realize what you are. It's that simple.

Our purpose is to be in alignment with what-is.

Fulfilling it is not easy. Letting go of thoughts is difficult. We typically need a lot of practice to do it. However, it really is that simple. The more you let go, the better your life will be.

You are already beyond form. You are what-is itself. There's nothing missing. Since you are complete, there's no need to look elsewhere or at another time for anything or anyone to complete you. A moment's realization is all that is required for you to glimpse a balanced life of wholly satisfying purpose. This explains why, as Roshi Kapleau reports in <u>ZEN Merging of East and West</u>, the Buddha exclaimed upon waking up, "Wonder of wonders! All living beings are inherently buddhas, endowed with wisdom and virtue." To be a buddha is to be awake. If so, the historical Buddha and many other sages assure us, we are already buddhas, already awake. It's just that the fog created by incessant thoughts is so thick that we can't see it.

Never to have glimpsed it is simply always to have suffered from ego delusion. The egoic mind is the problem. Dissolving it automatically removes ego delusion. With a thorough break-through, what's in store for you is not merely a few hours of happiness after which you return to normal. As long as you commit wholeheartedly to living the spiritual way, what's in store for you is abiding joy, equanimity, serenity, peacefulness and genuine love that can be indefinitely expanded or deep-ened. How could realizing your eternal nature be anything less? Why do you think that sages are always cheerful, smiling, hap-py? There's no such thing as a distraught sage.

Let's assume that this is correct. Let's assume that our pur-pose is simply to be fully human in the present moment, that all we need to live well is to drop thinking to kill the egoic mind and open to our eternal nature. Rene Char: "If you can dwell in one moment, you will discover eternity."

What, if anything, follows about what we should do? If our being is of infinite value, what value, if any, do our doings have? Let's consider the answer.

9

❖

Your Doing

What is the purpose (meaning, value, importance, significance) of what you do?

Every deliberate human act (action, behavior) actually has two values. Neglect of one of them is common and causes needless dissatisfaction.

One kind of value is intrinsic (internal, inner); the other kind is extrinsic (external, outer).

It's easy to illustrate the **extrinsic purpose**. Suppose that you are walking down a hallway to go to another room. What is the extrinsic purpose of the act of walking? That's easy: it's to get to another location. That other location is the other room. Obviously, that other room is something extrinsic to the walking itself.

It's the goal of the walking. It's what Aristotle called the "final" cause of the walking, its <u>telos</u> in Greek, which means its end.

Every act must have such an end (goal, purpose). All acts have teleological explanations. If it lacked one, you'd have no idea what to do and would be doing nothing. For example, if you didn't want to satisfy hunger or enjoy the taste of food, why would you eat? If you didn't want to get clean, why would you wash?

So getting to the other room is the extrinsic purpose of that episode of your walking down the hallway. You're not just walking aimlessly, wandering about with no destination. If someone asked you while you are walking a question such as "What are you trying to do?" or "Why are you walking in that direction?" you'd naturally answer by telling the interlocutor that you are trying to get to that other room.

This goes for all our acts. We don't just act randomly without reason. We act because we are trying to accomplish something, which is the act's extrinsic purpose.

What is the **intrinsic purpose** of an act?

It's unfortunate that it's easily ignored and often overlooked.

Distinguish an act's "what" from its "how." If you were asked while walking down the hallway, "*What* are you doing?" you'd simply reply that you are going to the other room. That satisfactorily answers the question. On the other hand, if you were asking, "*How* are you walking?" you might well be puzzled about how to reply.

One answer could be, "I'm walking with full attention to what I'm doing," in other words, you are not lost in thought but paying attention to what you are doing in the present moment. If that's true, your walking would be "mindful."

Actually, you probably would not be walking mindfully. You'd likely be thinking about what you are going to do in the other room once you get there. If so, you'd be walking distractedly, without paying conscious attention to your walking. You'd be taking the moments of walking to be merely means for doing something in the future in that other room.

Notice the imbalance. If you were walking distractedly while thinking about something else, you'd likely be thinking ahead. At least your thoughts would be separated from your walking. The implicit assumption you'd be making is that you'd be hoping that some future moment is more worthy of your attention because it might be better than the present moment. Do you understand the problem with doing this?

Whenever we do this, and we often do it, we are not fully

conscious of the present moment. We often fail to pay full attention to what's occurring now. Where's the problem?

The present moment is the only moment we ever have. Life only ever occurs in the present moment. Therefore, *to the degree that we fail to pay attention to the present moment, to the degree that we are lost in thought, we miss our lives.*

Dissatisfaction is created whenever our thoughts are about something other than the present moment. Again, dissatisfaction comes from separation. This is why ignoring *how* we do something while we are doing it is a terrible habit. It's ignoring the intrinsic purpose of our acts.

All deliberate acts have an intrinsic purpose as well as an extrinsic purpose. What is that intrinsic purpose? It's the same for all acts: it's to open time to eternity.

Other kinds of sentient beings such as other mammal species have no difficulty living in the present moment. As far as I can tell, unlike humans they don't have the ability to ignore the present by getting lost in thought.

That ability of ours is a precious gift. It's wonderful to be able to think well. Unfortunately, we frequently, almost constantly, misuse it.

Our distinctive purpose as human beings is to open time to eternity. (There are different ways to say this. For example, using 'our purpose is to open becoming to being' is the way I have usually written about it elsewhere. The terminological difference makes little difference.) We open time to eternity by focusing our attention properly. Paying full attention to the present moment without thinking is the correct way to focus attention.

Sometimes, of course, it's necessary to think. Sometimes, for example, there's an important problem to solve. Fine. Then think. If it's necessary to think, think; otherwise, develop the habit of paying full attention to the present moment, including and especially to what you are doing.

The reason sages tell us that we are often less than fully awake, as if we are dreaming our way through life, is because they notice that we are failing to pay full attention to the present moment. They notice that we are often lost in thought. It's a good analogy: going through life being lost in thought is like dreaming one's way through life.

It's not only possible to wake up from doing that, it's simple to do so. Again, 'simple' does not mean 'easy.' Not paying attention is an insidious habit. It's a difficult habit to break.

No matter: either we break it or we condemn ourselves to living poorly.

When we use the mind correctly, there is either minimal dissatisfaction or no dissatisfaction at all. This is why dissatisfaction is optional.

Using the mind correctly is balancing correctly between the temporal and the eternal. Living well is living such a balanced life.

This is a lesson that we are able to learn from nonhuman animals. Albert Einstein: "Look deep into nature, and then you will understand everything better." Why?

The primary reason we are unhappy is because we misuse the mind. Primarily that's because we live in the mind, particularly in our literate intellects as David Abram argues. Most humans live today in ways that suggest that they believe that we have little or nothing of value to learn from nonhuman animals. On the contrary, there's an extraordinarily valuable lesson that we can learn from them.

Recently, there was a great blue heron fishing in the shallow water of the lake in front of my house. I happened to see it. I watched it for about 15 minutes. It didn't have any luck and, so, it ceased fishing and flew off – presumably to try to find a better spot.

What was it doing? Fishing.

What else was it doing? Nothing! It was single-mindedly, wholeheartedly, doing what it was doing. It wasn't imagining how good a fish would taste for breakfast. It wasn't wondering why it's sometimes so difficult to catch fish. It wasn't feeling sorry for itself because it was having little luck fishing. It wasn't wishing it could be elsewhere. It was just fishing, paying full attention to what it was doing.

Eckhart Tolle tells of a Sufi master who, when asked how he woke up, said it was simply by watching how cats live when they are watching mouse holes and emulating them.

The *alert stillness* practiced by herons and cats and polar bears and frogs and many other kinds of animals is incompatible with dissatisfaction. **No unnecessary thought, no dissatisfaction.**

The critical mistake is to take each moment as nothing but a stepping stone to the next moment, taking the present as nothing but a means to the future. Let's consider a concrete example.

Suppose that you are hungry. You take some money to the market. Why?

To buy some food. Why?

To take it home. Why?

To cook it to prepare for eating. Why?

To eat it and make your hunger go away. It's a familiar sequence of events. There's nothing special about it. There's nothing wrong with what you do.

The problem comes with *how* you typically do it. When you are going to the market, it would be usual to think about what you are going to purchase once (and if!) you get there. When you are returning with the food, it would be ordinary to think about how you are going to prepare it and what you are going to eat with it. When you are preparing the food, it would be ordinary to think about enjoying it. When you are eating it, it would be ordinary to think about what you are going to do after eating. And so on. And on. And on – until death.

Alternatively, for example, when we eat we may also be conversing or listening to music or watching television. If so, the effect is the same since we are thinking about something else rather than paying attention to the present moment.

Notice how the mind is ordinarily focused on the next event or some other event. There's always another step, always something more to do, always something to consider doing in the future, always something else going on. *Focusing on the future or elsewhere draws attention away from the present.*

It probably doesn't seem like a big deal. However, what is doing something in the future? It's a thought. It's imaginary. It's not real.

Therefore, living this way entails that your **real experiences are infected by being in the service of unreal ones!** That is dysfunctional living, living poorly.

What's the alternative? Obviously, diminish or, better, drop thoughts about the future. Yes, it's important to plan what to do. If you want to eat, you'd better think about getting food. However, it makes no sense continually to contaminate present experiences with thoughts of future ones. The best way to have a good future is to have a good present. A good present is one that is lived fully, with little or no separation.

Whenever you set a future goal, just set it and forget it. Otherwise, you'll just be living the present in bondage to thoughts. Why continually live in bondage?

This is an everyday example of how, especially after we have acquired literacy to solidify our thoughts, we unintentionally become bound in our human-made surrealities. We get lost in a maze of distinctions and lose sight of the unity of the whole. Until we find our way home again, we remain stuck, hurting, dissatisfied. It's the price we pay for thinking too much, for living in thoughts.

Why not learn from nonhuman animals? Why not emulate them? When doing something, just do it. While doing it, stop thinking about anything else. Focus. Pay attention. Pay full attention. Make that a habit.

How can we learn to live like that? The same way we learn other skills or knacks: practice. **Practice focusing** all the time every day. Focus moment after moment after moment indefinitely. Master meditators are always meditating. They don't just focus during formal training periods.

Again, it's not either/or. It's little-by-little. The more we practice dropping excess thought, the more we become absorbed by the present moment. The more absorbed we are in the present moment, the more power we are drawing away from the egoic mind. The less power the egoic mind has, the weaker our self-concepts become. The weaker they become, the more we forget about self. The more we forget selfish worries, concerns, hopes, and plans, the more we open to everything else. The more we open to everything else, the more balanced our lives become and the better we live and feel.

Taming the egoic mind has its own rewards.[74] Do you have a persistent sense that something is missing from your life? If you have recently suffered an important loss, of course you do. However, as time passes almost always the hurt losses cause diminishes. We are adaptable. After struggling in various ways to adapt to loss, we usually manage again to turn down the volume on that sense of fundamental unease.

About twenty years ago my best friend Amy killed herself. Why? She was beautiful, kind, intelligent, well-liked, compassionate, well-educated, musically gifted, artistically talented, and young. It's not just that she seemed to lack nothing required for living well, she actually didn't lack anything required for living well. No matter: she didn't realize that. All her doings were insufficient. She suffered greatly and couldn't find an escape that worked. She knew something was really wrong, but the steps she took to correct the wrong by herself failed. She gave up hope.

These are heavy, serious reflections. Would you like a break from reading? Thinking well about living well is serious, but actually breaking through to living well results in plenty of laughter and lightness. Notice how much you enjoy a fit of laughing (a "laughgasm") that temporarily stuns all thoughts into submission.

Zen masters sometimes talk of a "samadhi of innocent delight" because after breaking through by dropping all thoughts it's possible, according to Yasutani Roshi, "to live with the spontaneity and joy of children at play."[75]

Would you enjoy watching videos by contemporary sages?

If so, my best suggestion is to go to YouTube and watch for free videos by spiritual teachers such as Eckhart Tolle. It'll likely take watching more than one to absorb any technical terminology and to adjust to a different delivery style, so be patient. There are lots of videos there that you may really enjoy and benefit from watching.

If you watch these, please keep the following question in the back of your mind: 'What should be my most important relationship?' Understanding that relationship is critical to understanding your purpose. That's what the next chapter is all about.

10

❖

Your Most Important Relationship

What's your most important relationship? It's <u>your relationship with whatever form(s) eternity takes in the present moment.</u>

Which forms do you identify with right now? Your body? Your thoughts? Your emotions? Your mood?

Whatever forms they are, they are all temporal. To identify with temporal form(s) is to be dysfunctional. If, as is almost certain, you do that, then your most important relationship is unbalanced, misaligned, off center.

If your most important relationship were not dysfunctional, you would be living well. If you are not yet living well, you have not yet balanced time and eternity. If you are living well, you are wholly at ease. Are you wholly at ease? It's unlikely.

The most important relationship is occurring right now. **Eternity is unfolding in time**. As Sengcan puts it: "one instant is ten thousand years."

Here's a central teaching from the Buddha:

"Let not a person run back to the past / Or live in expectation of the future; / For the past has been left behind / And the future has not been reached. / Instead with insight let him see / Each presently arisen state . . ."[76] The present moment has arisen. Forget past and future. Look at the present moment with insight. That means to take the emptiness of eternality to be the essence of whatever temporal forms are encountered right now.

DENNIS E. BRADFORD, PH.D.

Your relationship with the present moment will not be dysfunctional if you do not resist the insight that **emptiness is
the essence of each presently arisen form**. Your relationship with the present moment will be dysfunctional if you resist the insight that emptiness is the essence of each presently
arisen form.

The spiritual way is, in effect, to keep asking, moment after
moment, "What is my relationship to the present moment?"

It's not difficult to ask that question. What's difficult is re-
membering to keep asking it moment after moment after moment. What's difficult is to keep asking it with your gut instead
of your head.

If there is no inner resistance to the present moment, if you
do not mind at all what is happening, then you will be at ease.
Without resistance, there is no ego.

If, on the other hand, there is <u>any</u> resistance at all to the
present moment, if you do mind – even slightly – what is happening, then you are experiencing dissatisfaction that comes
from the egoic mind.

How do we detect resistance? In <u>A Separate Earth</u> Tolle
helpfully distinguishes three ways. Here are the three ways
your primary relationship becomes dysfunctional.

The most common way is taking the present moment as a
means to some better, future moment. As discussed in the previous chapter, the present moment is taken merely a stepping
stone to a preferred future. It's a way of trying to be elsewhere,
namely, in the future instead of the present. Obviously, this ignores the intrinsic value of the present moment.

Another way is taking the present moment as offering a
problem to be solved. It's just another obstacle to get past. Why
is this dysfunctional? Because another problem will immediately replace any solved problem; furthermore, there are some
problems that are insoluble. The Buddha told a farmer who had

complained to him about his problems, "If you work really hard on one of them, maybe you can fix it—but if you do, another one will pop right into its place. For example, you're going to lose your loved ones eventually. And you're going to die some day. Now there's a problem, and there's nothing you, or I, or anyone else can do about it" [From Steve Hagan's Buddhism Plain & Simple.].

The third way is taking the present moment as something that shouldn't even exist. It's an enemy that would be better off dead. The egoic mind has a better way for the world to be. This dysfunctional attitude leads to incessant complaining, blaming, hatred, and war. You've probably known people like that.

If your surreality is dysfunctional, your reality, your life, will be dysfunctional. The extrinsic reflects the intrinsic.

If your most important relationship is dysfunctional, what can you do about it? It's simple: pay full attention to the present moment and wholly accept it just as it is. In other words, focus on now and drop all resistance. Do this even just for a moment and you'll wound the egoic mind, you'll damage the ego. Keep doing it and you'll kill the ego. Why? You'll be dropping time and opening to eternity.

Here's the important insight: **without time, there is no ego**. To let go of time is to let go of the egoic mind. This is explains why the ego cannot abide the present moment for more than an instant and always flees it.

Again, thought requires time. No time, no thought. No thought, no egoic mind.

This explains why sages recommend dropping all thoughts, including all the thoughts related to your life story. For example, the Buddha says that a spiritual teacher who is attached to the thoughts that he or she is a self, a person with a life span and story is unauthentic. An authentic one "is not caught up in the idea of a self, a person, a living being, or a life span."[77]

To wake up is to give rise to "that mind that is not caught up in anything," in other words, it's "to give up all ideas." The requirement is not to detach from some ideas or thoughts but from *all* ideas.

A chief reason this is difficult is that we are afraid to do it. We think that if we stop clinging to thoughts we'll somehow disappear. We fear falling out of the world. After all, isn't emptiness the essence of every form? What would become of me if I were to realize my own essential emptiness? If I'm not temporal, then I'm only eternal, which entails that I am formless. In other words, we fear the emptiness of eternity.

There's no need. It's true that the essence of all forms is emptiness. That's as true for rocks, flowers, and tigers as it is for humans. Emptiness grounds everything. However, this insight is to be welcomed rather than feared. Why?

Emptiness is possibility. What, instead, if everything were permanent? Then nothing else would be possible! What-is would be a static plenum; it would be full.

Since emptiness grounds everything, everything (that doesn't involve a contradiction) is possible. Practice apprehending all forms as if their essence were empty. If you do, you'll soon begin to feel better. Why? You'll begin to realize that **every thing is everything else.** That's why we're never really lonely, separate, apart – we just think we are. We are really in communion with everything.

If it's true that everything is everything else, what do we lack? Nothing! How can we desire anything to complete us when we don't lack anything?

We don't realize how good we actually have it until we free ourselves from being trapped by thoughts. There's really nothing we have to gain or achieve or attain. There's really nothing we have to do. The way to realize that is simply to stop doing and just be. (Remember that thinking is a kind of doing.)

Perhaps not so incidentally, this undermines fear of death, too. Why? It's because nothing comes to be and nothing ceases to be. How could it? Are you able to think of even one form that came from nothing or that will become nothing? If emptiness really is the essence of all forms, how could a form be produced or destroyed? How could emptiness begin to be or cease to be? That's senseless, which is what Avalokita says to Shariputra in the sutra.

The law of (formal) identity applied to any form entails that it is what it is and it's not anything else. Logically, that's true. It's true only for the egoic mind. Actually, it's false: whenever we "look" deeply enough at any form, we see that it really is not itself in the sense that, if we truly understood it, we'd understand that it contains all other forms.

"No," you stubbornly object. "I am something."

Nobody denies that you are something. What the Buddha is famous (or notorious!) for claiming is only that you are not a self, not something separate. According to him, what we ordinarily think of as a self is nothing but a cluster of a human body, feelings, perceptions, conceptual fabrications, and cognizance (consciousness, awareness). These are qualities. None separately is a self. There's nothing personal here.

Words, concepts, and theories are endless. If all you do is think about the nature of a self, you'll just keep juggling concepts indefinitely.[78] The way to determine if the Buddha is right is to practice training (disciplining, purifying) thoughts in order to "see" better. Without such training, you'll just stay stuck.

The Buddha said, "Seeing in this way, as a trained practitioner, you become disenchanted with the body, feeling, perception, conceptual fabrications, and cognizance. Being disenchanted, you are free from infatuation. Because of this dispassion, you are liberated."[79] Doing that liberates us from the three poisons, namely, infatuation, hostility, and delusion, and enables clear insight into present-moment awareness that results in eradication, quenching, and unbinding, in other words, genuine freedom.

Lest you try to write all this off as strange Eastern philosophy, notice that Jesus also rejects attachment to self: "If anyone wishes to be a follower of mine, he must leave self behind . . ."[80] Detachment from self is not merely for the purpose of increasing one's happiness. Why? It's ethically critical. It erodes separation between self and other. As Jesus put it: "Love your neighbor as yourself."[81] Why? You are already in communion with your neighbor.

Detachment from self, from the egoic mind, cannot be accomplished by thinking about it. Superconsciousness requires detaching from *all* thoughts. That's the only way to salvation for ourselves and for others.

There's a further important consequence of this that I so far have failed to mention. Detaching from self undermines low self esteem, which is a major problem for many people (especially here in the west). Self esteem is how much or how little you like yourself. If you love or really like yourself, you have high self esteem. If you hate or really dislike yourself, you have low self esteem. There's a range and most people are somewhere in its middle.

One terrible consequence of having low self esteem is that it makes loving another well impossible. Why? It's a psychological law that it's impossible to love another more than you love yourself. So, if you have little self love, you cannot help but having little love for another. If you have little love for others, your relationships will never go well.

The cure is to drop attachment to self. After all, think about the oddity of the statement "I like myself" (or "I dislike myself"). Notice that there is the "I" doing the liking (or disliking) and the "I" or self being liked (or disliked). What sense does that make? Are you really two "I's" rather than one "I" or self? That seems very weird. How could that be?

You are not one self and you are not two selves. Whether you realize it yet or not, you are beyond the concept of self. You are both self and other. **You are beyond both form and emptiness.** There's nothing separating you except thoughts from realizing that you are everything and therefore you lack nothing.

Until we wake up, we live with false thoughts about ourselves. The best book I've read on the psychology of self-deception is Daniel Goleman's <u>Vital Lies, Simple Truths</u>.

Goleman argues that there are four sources of self-deception that we tend to ignore.

First, self-deception begins with perceiving. We ignore the many warnings given by philosophers and psychologists and find it easier simply to assume that our perceptions faithfully represent reality. They do not. To perceive is to select, in other words, to rule out a lot of perceptual information. This undoubtedly has survival value, but at least when we are in low-risk environments (as we usually are in North America), it's important to be more open-minded that we typically are. Why? Perceptions are constructions that are typically limited, distorted, and ill-formed (although they don't seem to be).

Second, the perceptual information that we select is distorted by our understandings, by the conceptual models we're attached to. This is actually a disadvantage in high-risk environments because, the more attached we are to our favorite conceptual models, the more distorted the perceptual information becomes and, so, the more likely we are to be injured or killed.[82] We can usually get away with it because, since our usual environment is low-risk, there's no serious consequence to the distortion.

Third, we are quick to commit the fallacy of hasty generalization. If we have a powerful positive or negative reaction to something, we have an unfortunate tendency to jump to the conclusion that all similar experiences will result in the same kind of positive or negative outcome for us.

Fourth, we confuse reality with surreality. We "confabulate." We like to assume that our thoughts about reality are accurate. No, reality doesn't contain any stories. It just is. The stories and explanations are our mental creations. Story-telling is our default format for understanding.[83] The problem is that we forget that we made up the stories and take them to be real.

As Roshi Kapleau writes in Awakening to Zen: "The mind of the ordinary person is a checkerboard of crisscrossing reflections, opinions, prejudices, fears, and anxieties, so that his life, far from being centered in reality, is grounded instead in his *notions* of reality." An ordinary person is a person who has yet to wake up. The good news is that all ordinary persons have the potential to awaken.

This is a critical reason why it's important to live an examined life. Without deliberately examining and countering these sources of deception, we begin to make decisions on their basis. Nothing is more toxic to living well.

Deliberately trying to live well is not difficult, but succeeding is difficult. Furthermore, your beginning to walk the spiritual path may threaten your friends and family who are trying just to hold things together rather than make life better. Living an examined life is stressful, and living among nonphilosophers is one of the main sources of stress.

Exposing yourself to novelty is stressful because it produces cognitive static, which staying on automatic pilot minimizes. Well, that's just the way it is. The way to get some good new ideas is to test a lot of ideas. Do what is required for living well or continue to live poorly until you die.

Goleman: "Learning to do something new requires full attention. It takes continual monitoring to absorb the task's requirements. The point of mastery comes when the task can be done without thinking about it, or with most of it on automatic."

To live well is to master life. To live poorly is to fail to master life. **You only have one life to live and there's no good reason not to master it.**

There's quite a lot that can be done about self-deception. You probably derive secondary benefits from doing nothing about it. Why not make a list of them and keep it ready-to-hand? Then whenever you are seeking an excuse not to do what you should be doing, pull out your list, find the excuse, and laugh at your timidity.

What's the cash value here? Master some spiritual or meditative practice. Question what-is with your gut and not just your head. Do whatever that requires. No matter that it's difficult: despite any physical pain, emotional distress, social isolation, or whatever else it costs you, persevere. Just drop all thoughts and keep dropping them. As the philosopher Nicolas Malebranche said, "Attentiveness is the natural prayer of the soul." Live attentively. Pay full attention. The Buddha's last words were "strive on untiringly."[84]

If you do, you'll adjust quickly enough to living well.

Waking up is the goalless goal of every classic spiritual practice. Again, it's an odd kind of goal since we already are awake, which means that the task is simply to uncover what's already there. In Awakening to Zen Roshi Kapleau writes: "The aim of Zen training is awakening, and the living of a life that is creative, harmonious, and *alive*. These [are] 'goal-less goals' for there really are no goals to attain, no place to get to . . ."

In other words, it's a mistake to practice with the goal of waking up. As John Daishin Buksbazen writes in Zen Meditation in Plain English, "let go of all ideas of 'making progress' or 'not making progress.'" Just practice being, not thinking. That means focusing on the suchness of the present moment.

Approach each moment as if **eternity is living me right now**. It is.

Realizing the nature that you already are means that you'll quickly adjust to leading a much more balanced life. Let's consider the idea of balanced, harmonious living.

11

❖

Balancing

Nothing is more important than opening to the eternal. At least since the beginning of the Axial Age that was the real beginning of civilization both in the east and in the west, the wise have been trying to get the rest of us to realize this. Our tendency is to get so caught up in our daily lives attending to forms that we forget that which is without form and that which is beyond form. We forget the eternal and focus only on the temporal.

The Upanishads are the oldest spiritual literature in human history. Over and over The Upanishads tell us that "the supreme goal of life" is realizing the eternal.

What I've here been labeling "the eternal" has many other names. A few of them are 'Being,' 'the divine,' and 'God.'[85] It's called 'Self' (with a capital 'S' to distinguish it from self) in The Upanishads. Since all words are forms and all forms are temporal, the words used make little difference. Use whichever word or phrase you prefer.

There are no words or concepts adequate to describe the eternal. All such words are nothing but signposts that should not be mistaken for what they point towards. In the Zen tradition, it's not infrequently pointed out that a finger pointing at the moon is not the moon and reading words on a menu does not satisfy hunger.

Mundaka Upanishad: "As long as we think we are the ego, / We feel attached and fall into sorrow."[86] The problem is that we cling to ego. The solution is to detach from ego and wake up. "The illumined sage is lost in the Self."

Similarly, the <u>Taittiriya Upanishad</u> says: "The wisdom sheath is made of detachment." How do we detach from the egoic mind and become wise?

It's by attending to the unitive stillness within. "[T]he ego and the Self dwell in the same body." So **we already are what we need to realize**. It's not as if the eternal Self is external to us. <u>Chandogya Upanishad</u>: "The Self is one, though it appears to be many." Let go of all the multiple forms to realize the eternal One.

The unitive Self is revealed through the stillness of meditation. It's not a matter of doing or achieving or gaining something. It's simply a matter of dropping all egoic attachments to accept reality just as it is in the present moment. It's a matter of releasing all separation.

No meditation, no detachment. No detachment, no wisdom.

Though it's true that "The Self is the source of abiding joy," this cannot be known by the thinking mind, by "the mere scholar" [<u>Taittiriya Upanishad</u>].

So **you are the eternal**. So we all are.

It's insufficient, however, merely to think that. The purpose of life is to realize it and live accordingly. **The purpose of life is to live in alignment with reality.**

If you don't yet believe that, that's only because you have not yet mastered some meditative practice.

One of the greatest books in the history of the world is the <u>Tao Te Ching</u>. The beginning of verse 16 is '<u>chih hsu chi</u>.' It means: "Attain complete emptiness. Cling to stillness." It literally means 'Cause complete emptiness.' Stephen Mitchell's translation is more helpful: "Empty your mind of all thoughts." Where does the 'your' come from?

Unlike English, written Chinese lacks grammar. Concepts are represented using pictures. Concepts are neither singular nor plural. There are no nouns, verbs, adjectives, nor adverbs in Chinese. There are no tenses (past, present, or future). Everything is perceptual.

By way of contrast, English has grammar. Events occur temporally – in past, present, or future – and temporal sequences are clarified. Subjects and objects are identified; their relationships are clarified. English does not have a perceptual context.

Obviously, then, translating from ancient Chinese to English is very difficult. Don't expect any definitive translations of any ancient Chinese texts into English.

The critical point is that 'complete emptiness' refers to mind devoid of thoughts, which is **alert, nonconceptual consciousness**.

'Attain' in 'attain complete emptiness' is misleading in the sense that, usually, attaining something is gaining something, which is the usual positive sense of attaining. Here it's the unusual negative sense of attaining that is relevant, the sense of letting go (releasing, surrendering).

The idea of clinging to the eternal can't be literally true because the eternal is formless. Stephen Addiss and Stanley Lombardo translate the recommendation as: "Hold fast to stillness."

The meaning is to open to the eternal and stay open to it. In other words, it's to break through to stillness and abide in it.

This change of perspective or **realization changes everything and nothing**. Someone who has had an initial breakthrough may not, for example, look any different although he or she may feel totally different.

Again, the opening to the eternal is capable of indefinite expansion or deepening. Breaking through initially isn't itself yet living well, but it can be the beginning of living well.

Although there are other ways to do it[87] and it can occasionally happen spontaneously, meditation is, by far, the most popular way to overcome compulsive thinking. It's the paradigmatic spiritual practice. The English word 'spiritual' comes from the Latin word used to designate breath or wind. While there are many different kinds of meditation, what they have in common is that they all focus awareness on the natural physical process of breathing.

I have in multiple other writings described how to do zazen, which is one zen way to meditate. The important point here is that there is nothing religious or supernatural about meditation. Since it's about not thinking, there's also nothing conceptual about it either. The basic idea is to pay such full attention to breathing that you let go of thinking.

Other spiritually effective practices such as aliveness awareness have a different focal point. So it's not necessary to focus on breathing as a way of letting go of thoughts; there are other alternatives.

Thoughts are mental noise. When we attach to them, they weigh us down. The task is not to identify with thoughts, but simply to notice them and let them go.

When?

Do you expect to wake up to stillness in the future after you have mastered a spiritual practice? That's just another thought. Now is the only time waking up is possible. **Awakening is now or never.**

The New English Bible, John 5:25: the time "is already here" for eternal life.

From The Gospel of Thomas[88]: "His disciples said to him: / "When will the dead be at rest?" / "When will the new world come?" / He [Jesus] answered them: / What you are waiting for has already come, 'but you do not see it.'"

Eternal life is available in the present moment. It's

available now. When else could it be available?

(Wordsworth's words form "Personal Talk" always resonate with me in such contexts: "To sit without emotion, hope, or aim, / In the loved presence of my cottage-fire.")

It's helpful to think of living a balanced life in terms of what we are, namely, human beings. The balance is between the human, which is temporal, and the being, which is eternal. As Eckhart Tolle writes in A New Earth: "Human is form. Being is formless. . . Mastery of life is . . . finding a balance between human and Being." He sometimes uses 'life' to mean the same as 'Being' or 'Presence,' which permits him to write: "I don't *have* a life. I *am* life." That shift is opening the temporal to the eternal. "The very reason for our existence in human form is to bring that dimension of consciousness into this world."

Where does this leave religious faith?

Let's follow Nietzsche here in his last book, The Anti-Christ, in which he makes a sharp distinction between Christ and his Christian followers.[89] 'Christ' denotes the Biblical Jesus ('Yeshua' in Aramaic; 'Yesu' in Greek and Coptic). In contrast to many of his followers, Christ's "genuine, primitive" religion was, according to Nietzsche, "above all a *not*-doing of many things, a different *being*."[90] That wasn't the object of Nietzsche's attack; rather, his attack was aimed at Christ's followers.

"'Faith' means not *wanting* to know what is true." Religious faith is a deliberate blindness. Nietzsche was, of course, like me, a philosopher, a lover of wisdom. The opposite of the probing, courageous open-mindedness of a philosopher is the deliberate close-mindedness of a fanatic. That's what Nietzsche is attacking. That's why he sums up his evaluations of Christians – not of Christ – by claiming that "Christianity has been up till now mankind's greatest misfortune."

He understood that Christ was not a hypocrite: "This 'bringer of glad tidings' died as he lived." Furthermore, he lived "to demonstrate how one ought to live. What he bequeathed to mankind is his *practice*."

Writing about Christ, Nietzsche states, "If I understand anything of this great symbolist it is that he took for realities, for 'truths', only *inner* realities – that he understood the rest, everything pertaining to nature, time, space, history, only as signs, as occasions for metaphor." So the bedrock of Nietzsche's evaluation of Christ is that Christ was true to his insight because he lived his inner realities.

What's most admirable in Nietzsche's evaluation of Christ is that he focuses on the critical concept, namely, the kingdom of God. Unlike many and probably most Christians, Nietzsche gets it: "The 'kingdom of God' is not something one waits for; it has no yesterday or tomorrow . . . it is an experience within a heart; it is everywhere, it is nowhere . . . "

He's not confused about the difference between eternal life and immortal life. He understands that the Pauline doctrine of the immortal soul ("The great lie of personal immortality") is a misinterpretation that "shifts the centre of gravity of life *out* of life . . ."

"Jesus . . . denied any chasm between God and man, he *lived* this unity of God and man as *his* 'glad tidings' . . ." In other words, heaven, the kingdom of God, is available here and now if one dissolves the separation between the human and the divine.

The divine is our essential emptiness that is obscured by our incessant thinking.

Furthermore, unlike many Christians, Nietzsche understands that Jesus does not think of himself as something special, that his unity with the divine was lived "not as a special prerogative!" In this sense, there was nothing unique about Jesus. Nietzsche wanted to shift "the centre of gravity of life" back into life from the "nothingness" where Christians – not Christ

– have banished it. The culprit for this was Paul, not Jesus, for it was Paul who "grasped that to disvalue 'the world' he *needed* the belief in immortality."

So Nietzsche's central critical claim is that it was Christians like Paul whose concept of the divine entailed that "God degenerated to the *contradiction of life,* instead of being its transfiguration and eternal *yes!*" Nietzsche wants to embrace life and say 'yes' to it rather than rejecting life and saying 'no' to it.

Isn't Nietzsche's criticism on target? Don't most Christians devalue "this" world in favor of otherworldliness? Hasn't Christ been misunderstood?

The eternal is the divine. The divine is the emptiness within each of us that is our essence. It's the stillness, the spaciousness, at the center of each of our tornadic forms.

If so, Jesus's divinity is no different from yours or mine. His salvation is no different than yours or mine. Again, what is critical is realizing this (by letting go of all thoughts) rather than merely thinking it.

There's no conceptual argument that could convince anyone here. The eternal is not divisible and, so, not conceptualizable.

There is a simple way, though, for any doubter to tell whether this conception is true, namely, find the still point. Open to the eternal. Drop all conceptualizing.

The claim that we are all essentially the same emptiness undermines all belief in being special. This is an ethically critical insight. Why? <u>A Course in Miracles:</u> "Specialness is the great dictator of the wrong decisions."

If you don't think of yourself as being special, then you think of others as being just like you. That means that there's no morally relevant difference between us. If all genuine love is Self [not self] love, then all others are one in emptiness with you.

If so, how could you hate or harm others? To realize that, as A Course in Miracles puts it, "You are not special" is to realize that other beings are as special as you. If so, how could treating others worse than you treat yourself possibly be justified?

If you harmed yourself, wouldn't you forgive yourself? Shouldn't you forgive yourself? If that other self harmed you, shouldn't you also forgive that other self? A Course in Miracles: "Forgiveness is the end of specialness."

The idea that we are all of equal moral worth is the idea of the brotherhood of all men. Setting aside the sexist language, it simply means that we human beings are all of equal moral value. By way of contrast, many people, including Plato and Aristotle, have believed that some people are special, that some people are of greater moral worth than other people. Once we accept that, then it's natural to think (as many, including Dostoevsky in Crime and Punishment, have pointed out) that we ourselves are special. If I think that I am special and you are not, my harming you may seem justified.

It's not.

We may desire to be special. We may think that we are special. We may convince ourselves that we are special. However, it's false that we are special.

Being special is self-created; it's false that it's Self-created. It's the work of the ego, whose initial work is separation, which then always turns into attacking and defending, which is the ego's main business. No separation, no ego. No ego, no attacking and defending.

There's no need to be special. Why? We already have an essence of emptiness, which is divinity itself. Each of us is divine. God is not somewhere outside the world; God is within each of us. So, as Jesus would put it, the kingdom of God is already here.

Immoral acts grounded on the idea of being special come from spiritual blindness. **The fundamental spiritual and moral**

reality is that we are all divine. So thinking of oneself as being special is a symptom of spiritual blindness. So, by the way, is thinking of some places as being holier than other places.

Spiritual blindness is not cured by arguments. It's cured by waking up. So, *the ethical imperative is: wake up!* It's not an accident that *the spiritual imperative also is: wake up!*

If you have ever seriously attempted it, it's not as easy to live a life of service to others as we tend to think. To ensure that you are not unintentionally making situations worse, first wake up and then help others. In Teachings on Love, Thich Nhat Hanh wisely advises: "Until we are able to love and take care of ourselves, we cannot be of much help to others. After that we can practice on others . . . " The Buddha says "that one who is himself sinking in the mud should pull out another who is sinking in the mud is impossible."[91]

As one student who had broken through is quoted as saying in The Three Pillars of Zen: "It is not selfishness to forget about saving others and to concentrate only on developing your own spiritual strength, though it may seem to be. The solemn truth is that you can't begin to save anybody until you yourself have become whole through the experience of Self-realization."

'Delusion disorder' is another name for spiritual blindness. Unfortunately, it's ubiquitous.

Where does it come from? How can it be cured?

We humans are aware of our limitations as animals. Although we don't know when it will occur, we know that we shall soon die. We are destined to become worm food, which seems to make a mockery of our grandest ambitions. We think ourselves the victims of a terrible hoax. Death undermines all our hopes and dreams. All our struggles to create valuable, purposeful, meaningful lives seem useless.

In response, we invent a fiction, namely, the reified concept of a self. This is the supposedly continuant substratum in which our qualities inhere. This is the separate self, and, of course, it's special.

Most people are not philosophers leading examined lives. Operating within a confusing maze of unexamined judgments is normal. Fundamental beliefs about the world are inherited from families and cultures and passed along from generation to generation. All egocentric understanding of reality is based on the fundamental presupposition that the reified concept of the self is real. It requires an intense, prolonged struggle to break free from this most serious delusion disorder and develop wisdom.

It's not just better thinking that is required. It's dropping thinking itself that is required. Nothing is more difficult. Nothing, though, is more valuable.

The common delusion disorder has consequences. In particular, the reified concept of the self has two primary consequences: antipathy (hostility, anger) and clinging (greed, attachment).

All dissatisfaction comes from these three sources, from delusion, clinging, and antipathy. This was a central teaching of the Buddha.

He says there is a way out. From The Dhammapada[92]: **"Meditation brings wisdom; lack of meditation leaves ignorance."** If you take only one idea away from this book, let it be that idea.

The wise are characterized by a nonegocentric attitude of compassionate nonclinging, in other words, an attitude of selfless giving or loving. They are the greatest lovers.

To become wise is to let go of the most serious delusion disorder. Doing this is waking up.

Anyone able to master any classic meditative or spiritual practice is able to do this and, although it is difficult, doing so is simple.

ARE YOU LIVING WITHOUT PURPOSE?

Do you want to become wise? Do you want to undermine all dissatisfactions? Do you want to become a great lover?

The good news is that you are able to do that. Nothing is forcing you to cling to the ideas of self and time. Dissatisfaction requires both time and self. No time, no dissatisfaction. No self, no dissatisfaction. Once pointed out (as I hope to have done clearly in this book), understanding what is required for living well is simple.

Now that you have understood how living well is possible, there's one critical question left about you: will you do what it takes?

Please remember that this is a "goalless goal." As Eckhart Tolle puts it in A New Earth, "You cannot make the egoless state into a future goal and then work toward it" by doing some spiritual practice. "The elimination of time . . . is the only true spiritual practice." This is phenomenological or psychological time that is characterized by "the egoic mind's endless preoccupation with past and future" and its unwillingness just to be in the present moment. Being conscious without thought, simply being still, dissolves phenomenological or psychological time.

What is spiritual practice? It's really nothing but allowing this present moment just to be as it is. Doing that dissolves time, dissolves self, and opens eternity. It's a conceptual solvent.

Waking up is being fully aware, which is what happens when all thoughts are dropped. It's what reconciles our primary purpose with our secondary purposes. Again, it's more about *how* we do what we do rather than *what* we do.

When we identify with our egos we attach to forms. When we do not identify with our egos we detach from forms. **Egoic attachment is pathological**. It's the paradigm of madness or insanity. Why? Again, it creates separation that is the root of all dissatisfaction. It's living discontently. **Egoic detachment**

is wisdom. It's the paradigm of living well. It's living peacefully.

It's important to note that this doesn't mean that you will stop enjoying the delights of this world, that detachment requires missing temporal realities, that you'll lose your "soul" if your "spirit" opens to the eternal. Not only will the delights of this world remain, but you'll actually enjoy them more fully once you begin experiencing them without clinging. To paraphrase Thich Nhat Hanh, practicing well is a very clever way to enjoy life.

I hope that you enjoy life fully.

12

❖

Next

Wchat should you do next? Without knowing you, nobody is able to provide rational guidance.

Again, living well is simple. Rather than living in
thoughts, it requires living in the real world at least most of
the time. Everyone needs an effective "practice" to get out of
thoughts and into life.

It's helpful to think of yourself as falling into one of three
classes: (i) you already have a practice that's working for you,
(ii) you are not yet ready to begin practicing, or (iii) you are
ready to begin practicing but don't already have a practice. My
suggestions for each follow.

If you already have a practice that's working for you,
why not intensify it? You may have come out of some spiritual
tradition or other for which you are well suited. If so, you are
quite fortunate. There's no reason to select a different practice.
If you need encouragement to intensify it, locate a master or
senior practitioner and get some advice from that person.

If you don't already have a practice that's working for you,
either you are not yet ready to select one or you are ready.

If you are not yet ripe to begin practicing, doing additional reading in some good related books or watching some
relevant videos may get you off the fence and into practicing. It
happens that I've read widely and deeply about this and may
be able to point you in a fruitful direction. I encourage you
to take seriously the suggestions in the "Reading and Video
Suggestions" below.

If you are ripe to begin practicing but don't already have a practice, I also encourage you to take seriously the suggestions in the "Reading and Video Suggestions" below.

If you are ripe to begin practicing, select some classic practice or other and start. It's impossible to know in advance which practice, or even which kind of practice, will work well for you. The task is to select one that you guess has a reasonable chance of working well for you and begin. If you quickly wonder where this practice has been all your life, which is the feeling I had as soon as I began zazen, then you will have luckily selected a suitable one for you quickly. If you don't get that feeling and give a practice a good shot, drop it and try another.[93] Remember that, ultimately, you'll drop any practice or technique you choose once you are routinely opening to the eternal.

If you are a beginner, you'll have a beginner's mind, which is good. On the other hand, you may not understand the biggest obstacle.

The biggest initial struggle you'll likely have is not in selecting a practice at all. The biggest initial struggle is likely to be with the ego, which doesn't want you to practice at all. For example, suppose you select a stilling meditation that requires practitioners to be still for relatively long periods of time. Your biggest initial challenge is likely to be pain. I find it helpful to think of such pain as sent by my ego in an attempt to get me to stop "sitting." Once it's accepted as just another egoic attack, it diminishes as a problem.

There's a trick here that may work: convince the ego that practicing will actually serve to make the ego more powerful. The ego is incessantly greedy for more power. Telling it that practicing will generate more power for the ego can fool the ego into thinking that practicing is not merely benign but actually beneficial for it. By the time the ego realizes otherwise, your practicing may have developed such momentum that it can't be checked by the egoic mind. Ego death may soon follow.

If you don't resist it in any way, if you fully accept it, no form can cause you to deviate from living the spiritual way. As Roshi Kapleau says in <u>ZEN Merging of East and West</u>: "nothing can menace your peace of mind if you become one with it." That goes for any kind of pain or distress. **Surrender fully to reality**. It may seem counter-intuitive, but doing that often makes any action you take to improve the situation more effective.

Finding a teacher who is both awake and knows you is a great blessing. How can you identify such a person? Here are some hints from Roshi Kapleau's <u>Awakening to Zen:</u> "The truly awakened are not argumentative, for they know that all statements are only half-truths, a looking from one side at that which has infinite dimensions . . . they do not regret the past, do not hope in the future, and are not dissatisfied with the present."

It need not take a lot of time to begin. What if you worked up to practicing for 20 minutes before breakfast and 20 minutes again late in the afternoon before dinner or just before going to bed at night? While 40 minutes would only be a small part of your 24 hour day, it would be sufficient to enable you to begin to live a more balanced life. That's how powerful proper practicing is. If you give up, say, watching a television show or two and instead practiced daily, you'll soon begin to realize for yourself how beneficial practicing is.

Remember the spiritual traps devised by the egoic mind. It's not all or nothing. Just as running is impossible for almost everyone without first learning how to walk, so living a life of purpose is impossible without first learning how to make life better and better.

Although it's true that the first moment of awakening marks a clear break from the more "unconscious" or "nonconscious" living that precedes it, it doesn't follow that the ground for waking up wasn't prepared. Here's a helpful way to understand that:

Recall that there is no mental activity, no (active) thinking, when practicing. There's just passive awareness (witnessing, watching, observing, detaching). You can decide to start witnessing right now. When else could you do it? The process is just to keep watching. Just keep witnessing. Become the silent, non-doing observer. As Eckhart Tolle writes in The Power of NOW, "The moment you start *watching the thinker* . . . You begin to awaken." As Osho puts it in Awareness, "Witnessing is the technique for centering." In other words, to find the balance point, the still center of the tornado or black hole that you are, begin witnessing. Then what? "Keep awareness there – let thoughts disappear." This is what meditation is: "When the mind is without thought, it is meditation." This works because "when the mind is gone . . . you can see that thoughts are not yours."

In other words, practicing undermines our natural tendency to identify with thoughts and other forms. Remember that every thought separates and "separation is the basis for the ego's sense of identity."[94] As soon as you stop identifying with thoughts, as soon as you realize that you are not your thoughts, you begin to feel oneness (eternity, Being, awake alert consciousness beyond form). So practicing identifying with the watcher helps to free consciousness from bondage to all physical and mental forms. Waking up, going beyond form and emptiness, also requires letting go of the watcher. The moment that that tips into fully awake (pure, formless) consciousness is **waking up**. Living that consciousness is living well.

Our primary purpose is not to seek salvation by doing something such as creating a better world. All such doings are secondary purposes. Instead, as Tolle puts it in The Power of NOW, our primary purpose is "to awaken out of identification with form."

It's not easy, but it's that simple. Since nobody is guaranteed tomorrow, if you have not yet made a start, it's important to begin If you don't begin to do it now, when will you ever begin to do it?

The answer is when changing becomes easier than staying the same.

That most often happens after an important loss. Someone you love deeply may die or dump you. You may lose your job or work. You may lose your house. You may lose your health or a body part or some bodily function. An important loss or similar situation can stimulate powerful negative emotions.

Doesn't that typically happen sooner or later to all of us?

When you are ripe, when you are really hurting, the silver lining is that you are most open to changing direction. A time of emotional vulnerability can motivate you to make changes that will improve the quality of your life for the rest of your life.

Understanding in principle why practicing is valuable is not the same as practicing. Reading articles and books like this one can be excellent preparation for practicing, but practicing itself is radically different. It's similar to the difference between reading about swimming or surf-boarding or sex and actually engaging in those activities.

Since we are in the middle of them, it's difficult to have perspective on our own lives. That's one reason why having friends is so valuable. A good counselor functions as a friend.

You may also find a free, self-assessment guide at my www. ConsultingPhilosopher.com website helpful. There are some other resources there, too, that you may find useful. Similarly, you may find helpful some of the hundreds of posts on my blog on well-being: www.Dennis-Bradford.com

Nobody needs to consult with me or anyone else in order to live well. *You already have everything required to live well.* On the other hand, if we didn't learn from each other, we'd still be living in caves. Reading some good works by others can really help, as can watching related videos. You'll find below some initial suggestions in the "Reading and Video Resources" section. Furthermore, nearly all my nonfiction books have a Suggested Readings near their end.

Before you get distracted doing things that seem more urgent but are really less important, you'd be wise to obtain some help from others to keep questioning what you are thinking, saying, and doing. The quality of those questions determines the quality of our lives.

The more dissatisfied you are, the more motivation you have to make changes. Getting help from someone who has been where you are and successfully worked out of it is an excellent procedure.

If you are not seriously dissatisfied right now, there's no reason to wait until your well runs dry to dig a new one.

Peace.

Dennis E. Bradford

❖

Terminology

C lear communication requires explaining technical terms (or ordinary terms used in technical ways) using ordinary terms. This section is designed to facilitate clear communication.

A **form** (object, thing) is whatever can be singled out (noticed, picked out, attended to, apprehended, focused on). It's anything that can be perceived, imagined, or conceived. Anything like that can also be remembered. A form may exist or not.

An **entity** (existent, real form) is whatever can be multiply singled out. It's the subject of a true material identity judgment.

A **predicative judgment** about one form has the logical structure "x is F" where 'x' is a variable ranging over particulars and 'F' is a variable ranging over qualities (commonalities, attributes, characteristics). For example, "this pen is black."

An **identity judgment** is either a "logical" one that has the form "a is a" or a "material" one that has the form "a is b" where 'a' and 'b' are variables that range over forms. A logical identity judgment asserts that a form is itself, whereas a material identity judgment asserts that two forms are one entity.

Material identity judgments are, if false, about two pure [isolated] forms; they are, if true, about one entity.

For example, if the pen that I am touching is the same as the pen that I am seeing, then there is one entity, one real pen. Although there may appear to be two pens (namely, the tactile pen and the visual pen), there is in reality only one pen that is simultaneously touched and seen. That's an example of a true material identity judgment. Notice that it's clear that there are two pure forms because, for example, while the tactile pen qua tactile form is colorless, the visual pen is colored.

For example, if the woman I am now looking at in the grocery store is not the same woman that I met at a party last month, then, despite what I may initially think, there are two women instead of one. In other words, it's false that the woman I am seeing in the grocery store is the same as the woman I remember meeting last month. Their appearances may be similar, but I would be mistaken if I identified them. That's an example of a false material identity judgment.

Once we realize that what we take to be an entity isn't one, once we realize that kind of mistaken judgment, we almost always lose interest. Why? We typically value entities and don't care about nonentities (except, sometimes, in certain ontological, mathematical, or logical contexts).

The entities that we value are typically continuants. A **continuant** is an entity that exists at two or more consecutive times. For example, your best friend is a continuant – and so is your automobile, your house, your favorite fishing spot, and so on. Not all entities are continuants.

What-is (reality, the world) is divisible into the temporal and the eternal.

The **temporal** is what is in time. It can be referred to in multiple ways. Some of the popular ones in English are the domain of: becoming, the many, the limited, noise, the finite, the relative, forms, thought, self, heaviness, dissatisfaction, aging, death, and ordinary happiness and unhappiness. It's also called samsara and dukkha.

The **eternal** is what is timeless. It can be referred to in multiple ways. Some of the popular ones in English are the domain of: Being, God, the divine, unity, the unlimited, the infinite, no-thought, lightness, peace, Self, Presence, silence, emptiness, the absolute, the formless, the kingdom of God, the unaging, the deathless, abiding joy, salvation, liberation, and the Oversoul. It's also called <u>nirvana</u> and <u>sukkha</u>.

The bifurcation of reality is the difference between the temporal and the eternal

A **concept** is a principle of classification, a way of separating (sorting, dividing, categorizing) forms. To **think** is to use concepts. A **thought** (judgment, proposition, statement) is an application of concepts. A **belief** is a thought we attach to as true. To **understand** is to think correctly; to misunderstand is to think incorrectly.

Consciousness is awareness. Consciousness may be conceptual or nonconceptual. Nonconceptual consciousness is direct experience without conceptual mediation.

Zen is a way of living, a practice, a method designed to help us live – and die – well. Though it has associated ideas such as the ones I've tried to explain in this book, it's not a creed or theory. Philip Kapleau, Roshi: "Zen is a religious practice with a unique method of body-mind training whose aim is awakening, that is, Self-realization."[95] Its only imperative is to wake up. Notice that he wrote "Self-realization" rather than "self-realization." The Self, which we all share, is our true essential nature, eternal emptiness.

A **buddha** is someone who is fully awake (from the root word '<u>buddh</u>' which means 'to wake up, to know, to understand'). **The Buddha** refers to the historical Buddha who lived about 2400 years ago.

The word '**ego**' is "a spiritually technical term for the delusive sense that oneself and the Universe are fundamentally separate."[96]

A Zen **roshi** is a venerable teacher.

To be **mindful** of a form is simply to pay full attention to it.

Endnotes

1. The New English Bible, Luke 17:20-21.
2. I offer a more complete account in Mastery in 7 Steps.
3. In case you are worried about it, the question about whether time is linear or nonlinear [circular] is irrelevant to this discussion. For example, illiterate humans in primitive cultures still experience the passing of time even though they may consider time itself as circular or repetitive. Partly because their languages may lack a word for the concept of time, it can be difficult to tell.
4. For more on Pascal and the importance of his ideas, see my blog post at: dennis-bradford.com/spiritual-well-being/blaise-pascal/
5. I discuss this much more thoroughly in Emotional Facelift. Its first chapter is available at the end of this book.
6. Encheiridion, Nicholas White, tr.
7. The Dhammadada, Easwaran, tr. Thich Nhat Hanh in Being Peace retells a story the Buddha told about a father and daughter in a circus that makes the point concretely.
8. I make the relevant critical point about ethics in Chapter 11.
9. Alagaddupama Sutta, Nanamoli & Bodhi, trs.
10. Khandhavagga, Bodhi, tr.
11. Mahavedalla Sutta, Nanamoli & Bodhi, trs.
12. Sagathavagga, Bodhi, tr.

13. The best answer I've yet come across to this question is in David Abram's <u>The Spell of the Sensuous</u>. Even if his diagnosis is adequate, however, he does not there give a healing prescription, which is what I am attempting to do in this book. I discuss his ideas more in Chapter 7.
14. I explain what this is and why it works in Chapter 8.
15. In <u>The Dhammapada</u>, Easwaran, tr.
16. <u>Opammasamyutta</u>, Bodhi, tr.
17. <u>Nidanavagga</u>, Bodhi, tr.
18. <u>Salayatanasamyutta</u>, Bodhi, tr.
19. In <u>The Diamond that Cuts Through Illusion</u>.
20. <u>Salayatanavagga</u>, Bodhi, tr.
21. <u>Bojjhaingasamyutta</u>, Bodhi, tr.
22. <u>Khandhasamyutta</u>, Bodhi, tr.
23. <u>Salayatanasamyutta</u>, Bodhi, tr.
24. <u>Malunkyaputta</u>, Nanamoli and Bodhi, trs.
25. <u>Maggasamyutta</u>, Bodhi, tr.
26. In <u>A New Earth</u>.
27. Compare, for example, <u>Awareness</u>.
28. <u>The New English Bible</u>, Matthew 27: 46-7 and Mark 15: 34.
29. <u>The New English Bible</u>, Luke 23: 46; compare John 19: 30.
30. <u>The New English Bible</u>, Luke 17:21.
31. <u>The New English Bible</u>, Luke, 21:19.
32. See Chapter 5.
33. <u>The New English Bible</u>, Luke 9:25.
34. All quotations from Sengcan are from the Rochester Zen Center's "Chants & Recitations."
35. I return to this in Chapter 7.
36. As I explain in Chapter 4, there can be, for example, perception without a thinker but not a thought (judgment, conceptualization) without a thinker.
37. I return to this in Chapter 7.

38. I spent six years in graduate school after four years as an undergraduate.
39. See my Love and Respect.
40. Vitakkasanthana Sutta, Nanamoli, & Bodhi, trs.
41. In The Power of NOW.
42. When my beloved wife of 14 years dumped me in favor of someone else, that forced me to admit that I was living much more poorly than I thought.
43. Udumbariak-Sihanada Sutta, Walshe, tr. That's what I think Jesus's 40 days in the wilderness were all about.
44. I myself started with t'ai chi and within months had dropped it in favor of zazen, which is the Zen kind of the spiritual way.
45. I recommend one in Chapter 12.
46. Upali Sutta, Nanamoli and Bodhi, trs.
47. Dvedhavitakka Sutta, Nanamoli & Bodhi, trs.
48. See Chapter 12.
49. Maharahulovada Sutta, Nanamoli & Bodhi, trs.
50. Sagathavagga, Bodhi, tr.
51. Nidanavagga, Bodhi, tr.
52. In The Dhammapada, Easwaran, tr.
53. Mahahatthipadopama Sutta, Manamoli & Bodhi, trs.
54. Karl Brunnhotzl, tr.
55. Incidentally, Red Pine has an excellent translation of, and commentary on, The Heart Sutra.
56. Quoted in The Three Pillars of Zen.
57. Madhupinkida Sutta, Nanamoli & Bodhi, trs.
58. Samanamandika Sutta, Nanamoli & Bodhi, trs.
59. Mahaparinibbana Sutta, Walshe, tr.
60. In Using Your Brain for a Change; his emphasis.
61. I picked up this idea from Gustav Bergmann, though it may not have been original with him.
62. I have discussed this problem elsewhere in multiple writings including Mastery in 7 Steps.

63. I picked up this idea from Osho, though it may not have been original with him.
64. Quoted in <u>The Three Pillars of Zen</u>.
65. Quoted in <u>The Three Pillars of Zen</u>.
66. Quoted in <u>The Three Pillars of Zen</u>.
67. In <u>A New Earth</u>.
68. A short, classic book I recommend on this is Eugen Herrigel's <u>Zen in the Art of Archery</u>.
69. Sengcan.
70. Sengcan.
71. Sengcan.
72. Roshi Kapleau in <u>Awakening to Zen</u>.
73. In <u>Involing Reality</u>.
74. There's a wonderful short book about this I recommend: Alan Cohen & Alan Gordon's <u>Are You As Happy As Your Dog?</u>
75. Quoted in <u>The Three Pillars of Zen</u>.
76. <u>Majhima Nikaya, 131, Bhaddekaratta Sutta,</u> Nanamoli and Bodhi, trs. Also see the beginning of the <u>Bhaddekaratta Sutta</u>.
77. From Thich Nhat Hanh's <u>The Diamond that Cuts Through Illusion</u>.
78. See Hermann Hesse's <u>The Glass Bead Game</u>.
79. In <u>Anattalakkhana Suttra</u>; <u>Samyuttankiaya</u> 3.22.59, G. Wallis, tr.
80. <u>The New English Bible</u>, Luke 9: 23.
81. <u>The New English Bible</u>, Matthew 22:39.
82. A good book on this is Laurence Gonzale's <u>Deep Survival</u>.
83. A good book on this is David R. Loy's <u>The World is Made of Stories</u>.
84. <u>Mahaparinibbana Sutta</u>, Walshe, tr.
85. See the Terminology section for more.

86. All translations here are by Easwaran.
87. dennis-bradford.com/spiritual-well-being/addiction-to-thinking-how-to-overcome it/
88. Jean-Yves LeLoup, tr.
89. R. J. Hollingdale, tr.
90. Nietzsche's emphasis.
91. Sallekha Sutta, Nanamoli & Bodhi, trs.].
92. Easwaran, tr.
93. I myself actually started with t'ai chi and in a few weeks dropped it in favor of zazen.
94. In Eckhart Tolle's The Power of NOW.
95. In Roshi Kapleau's The Three Pillars of Zen.
96. In Roshi Kapleau's Awakening to Zen.

❖

Reading and Video Suggestions

Emerson: "That book is good which puts me in a working mood."

If you've improved your understanding by reading this book and would like to take a look at more of my books, I've listed the relevant ones near the front of this book and in the end of the chapter 12 I've recommended other excellent resources.

Of course, it's possible to read books for free if you borrow them from a library rather than purchasing them. Here's a short list of books by others that have benefitted me and I recommend as especially suitable for beginners:

Anonymous, "Chants & Recitations" [Rochester Zen Center]

Kapleau, Philip, The Three Pillars of Zen

Osho, Awareness

Schucman, Helen, A Course in Miracles

Taylor, S. Waking From Sleep

Taylor, S. The Leap

Tolle, Eckhart, A New Earth

Tolle, Eckhart, The Power of NOW

If you happen to become interested in stilling meditation and have never done it, I have a video in which I demonstrate the easiest way for western adults to begin "sitting." It's easy to find on YouTube if you search for "kneeling meditation." It won't by itself help you still thoughts, but it may help you still the body and that's very helpful in stilling thoughts.

It's normal to be too stressed. Are you? If so, I have a private but free membership site *Mastering Stress* that contains half a dozen slide-show videos that you may find helpful. You may register at:

https://consultingphilosopher.kyvio.com/25867-enroll

(It typically will take a few minutes for your login credentials to be emailed to you. If you don't receive them after 10 or 20 minutes, check for them in your spam filter.)

There are plenty of excellent free videos available on YouTube that relate well to the topics in this book. Again, there are many excellent ones by Eckhart Tolle as well as by other spiritual teachers including my own teacher, The Venerable Bodhin Kjolhede, Roshi, and Thich Nhat Hanh.

A marvelous source of audio recordings of <u>teisho</u> talks, videos, and streaming podcasts that may help you practice or enhance your practice is available at no cost at rzc.org [the Rochester Zen Center website] under the 'Teachings' tab at the top of its homepage.

An excellent paid resource I wholeheartedly recommend for those nearby is a one-day training at the Rochester Zen Center that occurs on a Saturday about 7 times yearly. See their website at rzc.org for details. It's excellent training and a delicious lunch is included. There are no more than about 50 participants. It's $60. (If it's difficult for you to afford it, there's an Abbot's fund available that may be able to help.)

I wish you all the best.

------------ ❖ ------------

About the Author

Dennis E. Bradford is extremely well-qualified to write about the purpose of life. You have found a guide who as "been there and done that!"

Education and Teaching Experience:

- Over 55 years experience as a philosopher, a lover of wisdom
- Diploma from Blair Academy
- B. A. in philosophy from Syracuse University
- M. A. and Ph.D. in philosophy from The University of Iowa
- 32 years experience teaching philosophy and humanities full-time at the State University of New York College at Geneseo
- Studied and taught all the major philosophers from both the Western and Eastern philosophical traditions
- Zen practitioner since 1994.

Publications:

- 29 books [including 6 works of fiction under pen names]
- Multiple articles [including 20 articles at my.ezinearticles.com]
- Several hundred blog posts on well-being at www.Dennis-Bradford.com
- Multiple websites including: www.ConsultingPhilosopher.com

Personal Information:

- Former member of MENSA
- Former member of the American Philosophical Association
- Amazon bestselling author
- Many years playing in the Rochester Metro Hockey League
- 2 years as a lieutenant in the U. S. Army with overseas duty in Korea
- Lives peacefully in solitude in his home on the shore of a Finger Lake in upstate New York
- Volunteers weekly leading a meditation group at a nearby prison
- Amazon Author Central page:
  https://www.amazon.com/Dennis-E.-Bradford/e/B0047EI11A/

❖

Bonus Chapter

[H]ere's the Preface to the Reader from my new book EMOTIONAL FACELIFT Understanding Liberation from Negative Emotions Without Doing Time in a Monastery!, which is an excellent companion volume to this book. (I've eliminated endnotes here.)]

If you are an experienced fisherman, you have learned that fish like structure. Instead of preferring to be exposed to predatory larger fish, they prefer to be in or near underwater structures such as weed beds, drop-offs, logs, or human artifacts such as sunken boats or ships or at least to be in schools of related fish. Isolated fish are simply in more peril.

Our minds are like fish in the sense they prefer thoughts that are related to or thoroughly embedded in other thoughts. The phrase 'emotional well-being' is complicated in the sense that it involves not only two concepts (namely, the concept of an emotion and the concept of well-being) but lots of other thoughts to which it is related. After all, the way that we understand something is never as an isolated object but rather by noticing its similarities and differences to other things.

My purpose is to encourage you to detach from any beliefs about emotions that are obstructing your emotional well-being (your living well emotionally, your flourishing emotionally). Yes, it's only theory, but it's important theory. Why? Once your thoughts about emotions are aligned with reality you'll be able to begin to practice emotional well-being.

Once you begin practicing properly, the quality of your emotional life will quickly improve.

Until you question the beliefs about emotions that you already have and eliminate the obstructive ones, you'll simply stay stuck emotionally. Your emotional life will *never* significantly improve. It's false that emotional well-being happens accidentally. Therefore, if you want your emotional life to improve significantly, then you've no choice but to examine your beliefs about emotions, discard those you find wanting, and replace them with better ones.

Once you regularly begin thinking better about emotions, with some practice you'll quickly begin feeling better emotionally. For example, if you are suffering acutely right now from grief, anger, fear, loneliness, or any other negative emotion or cluster of negative emotions, you may **hope** again that you need not stay stuck, that emotional freedom really is a genuine option for you.

The reason that's the case is because there's a very important difference between thinking about emotional flourishing (excellence, well-being) and, say, thinking about physical flourishing (excellence, well-being).

Suppose that you have a whole body that is neither injured nor diseased. Suppose, too, that you are obese and that you want to free yourself from that condition. So you go to your personal physician for an examination and a plan of action that includes eating well and exercising well. As long as you believe that your physician is an expert, you do not have to have a sophisticated understanding of physiology to carry out that plan. That's good – otherwise, you would also have to go to medical school or at least do a lot of reading and studying to become an expert yourself before being able to lose body fat. Fortunately for you, it's possible to lose a lot of unwanted body fat by following an expert's advice even if you do not understand why the expert gave you that advice.

The reason for that is because your *thoughts don't determine your percentage of body fat.* Instead, it's your genetics and environment (including your eating and exercise habits) that determine your percentage of body fat.

The reason for the dissimilarity between emotional flourishing and physical flourishing is that your **thoughts do determine your emotions.** As I argue in what follows, emotions essentially are thoughts. So improving how you think about them can have a direct, positive effect upon your degree of emotional well-being.

It's wise to be skeptical about this. In fact, it's wise to be skeptical of all my claims; you'd be a fool not to doubt them. Please treat all my statements as if they were questions. After all, others have misled you before, haven't they?

If the evidence I marshal in favor of my claims is as strong as I believe it is, then your skepticism will quickly fade.

On the other hand, it's important not to be negative. For example, if you are attached to the belief that nobody flourishes emotionally, all you are doing is guaranteeing that you will never flourish emotionally and never enjoy any significant emotional improvement. Those who are stuck being fools are stuck being fools.

In other words, you must be open to improving your understanding to benefit from reading this. If you are close-minded, I cannot help you live better emotionally. Why? Nobody can help you live better emotionally; furthermore, you won't even be able to help yourself.

So, if you are serious about living better emotionally, please detach from whatever beliefs you have right now about emotions. Just set them aside for now. Open your mind by challenging them. If you accept the ideas presented here, then you can discard those old ones permanently and replace them with better ones. If you do not accept the ideas presented here, then you can always go back to your old ideas.

Please examine your own beliefs. At least when it comes to emotional flourishing, please question how you think about emotions.

I happen to believe that the only way to live well is to live an examined life. The reason for that is that living well (living wisely, mastering life) never happens accidentally or magically. It's always the result of a deliberate process. Living well is difficult; it's not easy. If we want to live well, we need to examine the alternatives to select the most suitable one.

Except for laziness, there's no reason not to live an examined life. If examination reveals a better way to live, then you'll obviously have benefitted from your examination. If it doesn't, you'll still have benefitted from your examination because at least you'll understand better why certain options are poorer than what you are now doing and you won't need to change what you are already doing.

There are two kinds of methods for emotional flourishing, the proactive and the reactive. Although I recommend both, I only consider <u>the reactive method</u> in what follows. Let's suppose that you are reading this because you are in the grip of some powerful negative emotion and want to free yourself. (There are other good reasons for reading it. For example, even if you feel fine now, you realize that good fortune may not always smile upon you and life will sooner or later hit you with situations, related either to yourself or to loved ones, such as aging, illness, and death that may leave you suffering from a powerful negative emotion or even from more than one simultaneously.) If so, realize that your ability to concentrate is diminished by your current emotional condition. So be very patient with yourself as you gradually absorb the ideas presented here; it simply may take you longer than normal to understand them. I encourage you to read this slowly at least twice.

An inability to concentrate is a common trait of powerful emotions: when we are seized by one, our range of focus narrows. The more powerful the emotion, the more our range of focus typically narrows in the sense that it becomes more and more difficult to think about anything else.

It feels really good to be able to focus single-mindedly on whatever we choose. Someone who lives well emotionally always has that ability. When we become absorbed in some task, we perform it better than we otherwise would. Furthermore, time-consciousness and self-consciousness temporarily vanish as we actually become what we are doing. That kind of focus is characteristic of mastery.

Unfortunately, you were not educated as a child about emotion well-being. Nobody explained to you either how to reduce the frequency with which you are afflicted by unwanted emotions or how to get rid of them when you suffer from them. The result is predictable: **few people flourish emotionally**. As you are probably aware, lots of adults look good and smell good but their thoughts and emotional lives are chaotic and unsatisfying.

Learning how to flourish emotionally is part of learning how to master life. Mastery requires full attention. Acts performed with only partial attention bring little reward. If you decide that something is worth doing, do it while paying full attention. The Buddha: "If anything is worth doing, do it with all your heart."

You have the ability to **master life**. Yes, it's **difficult**. It takes the right kind of practice over an extended period of time. On the other hand, it's so **simple** that any normal human being can do it. It doesn't even require literacy. By the time you finish reading this, I hope to have explained clearly why that's the case.

You are a normal human being. That's true even if you happen to be suffering acutely right now. So, please don't despair.

There are two tasks that confront you. First, assuming that you are hurting emotionally, get back to normal emotionally. What you learn here will help you to do that. There's no good reason not to transform acute emotional distress into emotional normalcy. If it's available to you, consider getting some help from a psychiatrist or clinical psychologist to resume normalcy. Second, once you are normal again, don't stop the progress. Keep going. There's no reason to lead a "settle for" life. Don't settle for just living normally emotionally. Unless you unnecessarily and foolishly attach to the belief that you are unable to do it, there's no reason that you cannot live well emotionally. There's no good reason not to transform emotional normalcy into enjoying emotional freedom, living well emotionally. Don't worry: there are books like this one and guides, perhaps including me, who can help you do that.

In fact, if you are ripe for it, you may be astounded at how quickly that can occur. The more determined you are to diminish or eliminate emotional suffering, the more motivation you have to do it. That's the consolation hidden within what might be almost suicide-inducing emotional suffering. After you finish reading this book and absorbing the ideas presented here, how fast might you be able to dissolve *any* negative emotion that is troubling you? It may take just an hour or two! Even if it were to take you a day or two or even a week, so?

The real value of learning about emotions isn't having improved thoughts: it's using that improved thinking to improve the quality of our emotional lives.

There's an added important benefit in addition to the obvious one of reducing or eliminating emotional suffering: mastering emotions will give you practical experience with respect to what is required for mastering life. **Mastering emotions is a gateway to mastering life**.

"In order to swim, one takes off all one's clothes – in order
to aspire to the truth, one must undress in a far more inward
sense, divest oneself of all one's inward clothes, of thoughts,
conceptions, selfishness, etc., before one is sufficiently naked."
--Soren Kierkegaard

When you are ready to strip down and get going, please continue.

www.ingramcontent.com/pod-product-compliance
Lightning Source LLC
Chambersburg PA
CBHW060312050426
42448CB00009B/1795